ALASKA'S

Natural
WONDERS

A GUIDE TO THE PHENOMENA
OF THE FAR NORTH

Robert H. Armstrong & Marge Hermans

ALASKA NORTHWEST BOOKS™

ACHNOWLEDGMENTS—Many people helped us by providing information through interviews, sending publications, or editing the manuscript and selected articles. We especially thank Richard Gordon and Roger W. Pearson, who reviewed early drafts of the entire manuscript. We would also like to thank Natalie Abrams, Greg Balough, Kurt Byers, John Byler, Richard Carlson, Richard Carstensen, Deb Coccia, Cathy Connor, Jan Dalrymple, Mark Daughhetee, Neil Davis, Jo Engleberger and members of the Internet nature writing workshop, Robert Hodge, Elizabeth Hooge, John J. Kelley, Linda Kienle, Matt Kirchhoff, Elizabeth Knecht, Charlie Lean, Carol Lewis, Beth Mathews, Barry McWayne, Roman Motyka, Chris Nye, Tom Osborn, Tom Osterkamp, Mark Oswood, Penny Rennick, Mark Schwann, David B. Stone, Pauline Strong, Jerry Super, Julia Triplehorn, Rose Watabe, Mary Willson, Bob Wolfe, Kat Woods, Kes Woodward. Special thanks to Ellen Wheat, who first envisioned this book, and Don Graydon, whose careful editing improved our writing.

Text © 2000 by Robert H. Armstrong and Marge Hermans
Book compilation © 2000 by Alaska Northwest Books™
An imprint of Graphic Arts Center Publishing Company
P.O. Box 10306, Portland, Oregon 97296-0306; 503-226-2402
www.gacpc.com

Library of Congress Cataloging-in-Publication Data
Armstrong, Robert H., 1936–
    Alaska's natural wonders / Robert H. Armstrong and Marge Hermans.
      p. cm.
    ISBN 01-88240-526-8 (alk. paper)
    1. Natural history—Alaska. I. Hermans, Marge, 1942– II. Title.
QH105.A4 A84 2000
508.798—dc21   99-055671
                                                                CIP

PHOTOS—*Front cover:* Aurora borealis over Mount St. Elias, © Norio Matsumoto; *Back cover:* Hubbard Glacier, © Mark Newan/AlaskaStock.com; *Pages 1–2, 95–96:* Hubbard Glacier calving into Russel Fiord, © Karen Jettmar/AlaskaStock.com; *Page 3:* Downtown Anchorage with Mt. Spurr erupting in the background, © Bob Hallinen/AlaskaStock.com; *Page 5:* Humpback whale breaching, © John Hyde/AlaskaStock.com; *Pages 12–13:* Mount McKinley, © Patrick Endres/AlaskaStock.com; *Pages 48–49:* Steller sea lions, © John Hyde/AlaskaStock.com; *Pages 80–81:* Aurora borealis over Alaska Range, © Johnny Johnson/AlaskaStock.com.

President/Publisher: Charles M. Hopkins
Editorial Staff: Douglas A. Pfeiffer, Ellen Harkins Wheat, Timothy W. Frew, Tricia Brown, Jean Andrews, Alicia I. Paulson, Julia Warren
Production Staff: Richard L. Owsiany, Susan Dupere
Designer: Constance Bollen, cb graphics
Editor: Don Graydon
Map Artist: Gray Mouse Graphics

Printed on acid- and elemental-chlorine-free recycled paper in the United States of America

Contents

A Land of Wonders

The natural wonders of Alaska are startling in their scale and profusion. Alaska is the only state with pack ice, midnight sun, and extensive permafrost. It encompasses entire mountain ranges, a coastline bordering two oceans and three seas, and a chain of islands 1,400 miles long. It extends across so many degrees of latitude that it contains both temperate rain forests and arctic tundra.

To visit Alaska or to live in the state is a wonder in itself. As residents of Juneau, we live with a glacier in our backyard. We hike through forests hundreds of years old, and we share our woods with brown bears and our inland waters with whales. Within the state we can fish in wilderness rivers, walk on cushiony tundra, or thrill to the aurora borealis on cold winter nights.

In the pages of this book, we explore the most remarkable natural features of Alaska. These are the glaciers and volcanoes and other phenomena that in magnitude and abundance set Alaska apart from the rest of the United States, North America, and the world.

Wonders such as permafrost, pack ice, and the midnight sun result from the northerly location of Alaska—the only U.S. state that stretches into the Arctic. Yet Alaska's great size and expanse permit a spectacular diversity of natural marvels.

Distance from large population centers has kept many of these natural wonders natural. Equally important, many of them lie within huge areas of protected lands. A total of about 143 million acres of parklands—a third of Alaska's land, including tidelands—provide the setting for most of the state's natural wonders. Parklands in Alaska include two-thirds of the acreage devoted to the nation's national parks, monuments, and preserves; 83 percent of all land in national wildlife refuges; a third of all U.S. parklands

Otter Lake in
Southcentral Alaska.

Prince William Sound, Southcentral Alaska.

under state administration; and more than half of all designated wilderness in the United States.

Many of these parklands are unusual in that, unlike in most other parts of the United States, they encompass ecosystems that are relatively intact. They are places where we can still see "all the parts" operating naturally. Alaska has the last major free-roaming populations of wolves, brown bears, mountain goats, wolverines, caribou, and moose. More bald eagles, loons, marbled murrelets, salmon, and arctic grayling live in Alaska than anywhere else. These animals fare poorly near civilization and require the extensive landscapes, freedom from human contact, and pollution-free environment that much of Alaska provides.

Maintaining natural communities untrammeled by human impact grows more difficult by the day, however. Wild areas once shielded by their relative inaccessibility are no longer out of reach in an age of helicopters, floatplanes, snow machines, and high-tech outdoor gear. Even in the most remote areas, visitors are quite likely to meet other travelers or to find evidence of people who came before them.

In writing about Alaska's wonders, we selected facts and facets we find unusual or especially interesting—fascinating details that make us all sit up and maybe even gasp a bit. We also show how these wonders relate to their surroundings, how they work, and where they came from.

Every wonder we describe can be seen along fairly common routes of travel, as noted briefly under "Where to See It" in each section of the book. More extensive travel information can be found in the excellent guidebooks listed under "Suggested Reading" at the back of the book.

Included with many topics is a short "Conservation Note" calling attention to issues that could affect the ability of future generations to enjoy what seems so wondrous to us today. Alaska shares in the effects of global climate change, air and water pollution, growing world population, and the expansion of tourism. As part of the world's environmentally sensitive polar region, Alaska could feel these effects relatively quickly and drastically.

Like most people who visit or live in Alaska, we are fascinated by its magnificent array of natural wonders. We offer this pocket guide in the hope it will add to your enjoyment and appreciation of these masterworks of nature and thus help to assure their preservation. ■

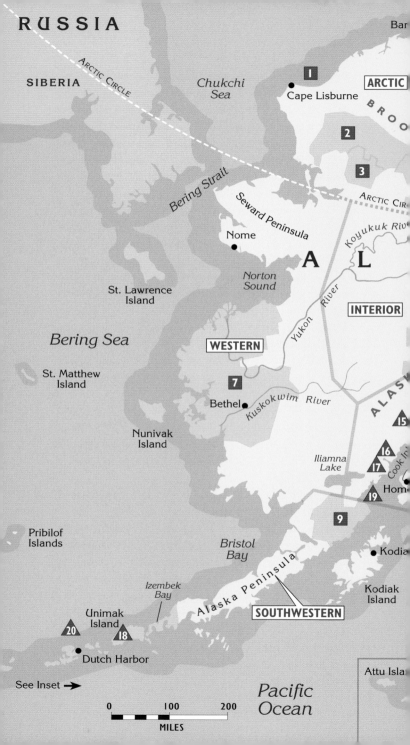

Arctic Ocean

Prudhoe Bay

Beaufort Sea

DALTON HIGHWAY

RANGE

5

Porcupine River

Fort Yukon

6

Circle

S K A

Elliott Hwy

STEESE HIGHWAY

Yukon River

Fairbanks

ana

Tanana River

ALASKA HIGHWAY

TAYLOR HIGHWAY

TOK CUTOFF

RANGE

DENALI HIGHWAY

GLENN HIGHWAY

WRANGELL MOUNTAINS

RICHARDSON HWY

14

EDGERTON HWY

10

ST. ELIAS RANGE

Anchorage

Valdez

Cordova

SEWARD HIGHWAY

Prince William Sound

Kenai Peninsula

CANADA

Chilkat River

Haines

Juneau

Taku River

COAST MOUNTAINS

Yakutat

11

SOUTHCENTRAL

Gulf of Alaska

Admiralty Island

12

Petersburg

Wrangell

Sitka

SOUTHEAST

Ketchikan

Prince of Wales Island

I

Aleutian Islands

I

SOUTHWESTERN

Queen Charlotte Islands

N

UNITED STATES

CANADA

1. Alaska Maritime National Wildlife Refuge (includes entire coastline)
2. Noatak National Preserve
3. Kobuk Valley National Park
4. Gates of the Arctic National Park and Preserve
5. Arctic National Wildlife Refuge
6. Yukon Flats National Wildlife Refuge
7. Yukon Delta National Wildlife Refuge
8. Denali National Park and Preserve
9. Katmai National Park and Preserve
10. Wrangell-St. Elias National Park and Preserve
11. Glacier Bay National Park and Preserve
12. Admiralty Island National Monument
13. Mount McKinley
14. Mount Wrangell
15. Mount Spurr
16. Mount Redoubt
17. Mount Iliamna
18. Mount Shishaldin
19. Mount St. Augustine
20. Bogoslof Volcano

BIOGEOGRAPHIC REGION BOUNDARY

LAND

Volcanoes

The island is like a live thing, its knots and ropes of muscle petrified into black rock. It's heaped into mounds, ledges, and cliffs—remnants of some ancient outburst now being soothed, smoothed, softened by the waves.

—Marge, on volcanic island off Sitka

More than 40 active volcanoes simmer within the borders of Alaska. That's 80 percent of all active volcanoes in the United States. Since World War II, 23 of them have erupted, some violently and repeatedly.

Mount Augustine during 1986 eruption, Southcentral Alaska.

Rather than discharging large quantities of flowing lava, Alaska volcanoes typically eject clouds of explosive gases and ash. The ash clogs the air, blocks the sun, and irritates eyes and lungs. Finer than sand, the ash consists mostly of sharp, angular fragments of volcanic glass.

Most Alaska volcanoes are located along a 1,550-mile arc that extends from Hayes Volcano (90 miles west of Anchorage), along the Alaska Peninsula, and westward through the Aleutian Islands.

The 1,400-mile-long Aleutians are actually the tops of submarine volcanoes. Mount Shishaldin, highest point in the Aleutians, rises more than 32,000 feet from the ocean floor, but only its top 9,372 feet are above sea level. Shishaldin has erupted at least 28 times since 1775, including major explosions and ash emissions up to 45,000 feet above sea level in April 1999.

Alaskans have been watching Bogoslof Volcano, Alaska's newest, create a changing mass of pinnacles, cliffs, and rocky islands for well over a century. In 1796 Russian-American Company workers on Umnak Island in the Aleutians reported three days of earthquakes, falling pumice, and brilliant flames near what Captain Cook in 1778 had named Ship Rock, 60 miles west of Dutch Harbor. Since that time, at various intervals, so many different domes and spires of rock have emerged, collapsed, and eroded around the volcano it has been nicknamed Jack-in-the-Box.

Four active volcanoes lie within the Cook Inlet region: Mounts Spurr, Redoubt, Iliamna, and Augustine. They are of special concern because of their proximity to the urban areas of Anchorage and the Kenai Peninsula, where half the state's population lives. Like the Aleutian volcanoes, they are within the North Pacific flight path. More than 10,000 airline passengers a day and most of the air cargo between eastern Asia and North America travel close to them.

Mount Redoubt, only 105 miles southwest of Anchorage, has erupted five times since 1900. In December and January 1989–90, eruptions spewed ash more than 7 miles into the air, brought darkness at noon to Kenai and Soldotna, short-circuited electrical transformers, and disrupted air traffic. On December 15 a Dutch

THE TERRIBLE TRIO:
VOLCANOES, EARTHQUAKES, AND TSUNAMIS

ALASKA'S ENTIRE SOUTHWESTERN COAST extends along the fault where the Pacific oceanic plate and the North American continental plate meet, and that is where most of Alaska's numerous volcanoes have formed.

The tremendous pressures created as plates move in relation to each other also cause earthquakes. Alaska has more earthquakes than the rest of the United States combined. Many of these events are small and affect only remote areas, but 3 of the world's 10 largest earthquakes since 1904 took place in Alaska.

The Good Friday earthquake that struck Southcentral Alaska in 1964 was the second-largest ever recorded on earth. It displaced some 100,000 square miles of the earth's crust and caused $330 million damage. Downtown Anchorage was devastated as portions of Third and Fourth Avenue dropped as much as 10 feet. Landslides and massive slumps affected large areas of the city, and a 130-acre landslide in the Turnagain area destroyed 75 homes. In Valdez, 120 air miles east, the entire waterfront disappeared in a massive submarine slide, while the waterfront in Cordova, 50 miles farther south, was uplifted six feet, leaving the boat harbor and cannery docks above all but the highest tides.

Earthquakes, the slides they cause on land or beneath the ocean, and flows of volcanic material into the sea can create tsunamis. These powerful waves can travel across the ocean at almost 600 miles an hour, rising nearly 100 feet high when they approach shore. Tsunamis generated by the Good Friday earthquake caused more than

airliner bringing 244 passengers and crew to Anchorage encountered an ash plume downwind from the volcano, lost power in all four engines, and plummeted 13,000 feet in a matter of seconds. The pilot succeeded in restarting the engines only 6,500 feet from the ground.

Katmai National Park and Preserve, at the northeast end of the Alaska Peninsula, marks the site of the largest volcanic eruption of this century and one of the most violent ever recorded. The eruption in 1912 of Novarupta Volcano on the flank of Mount

Portions of downtown Anchorage dropped as much as 10 feet during the 1964 Good Friday Earthquake.

---

90 percent of the 131 deaths attributed to the quake. They devastated the waterfront at Kodiak and destroyed the village of Chenega in Prince William Sound, killing 23 of its 72 inhabitants and leaving only the school building standing.

Because of the hazards they pose, volcanoes, earthquakes, and tsunamis are closely monitored in Alaska. Responsible agencies are the Alaska Volcano Observatory and the Alaska Earthquake Information Center, both with offices in Anchorage and Fairbanks, and the West Coast/Alaska Tsunami Warning Center, in Palmer. ■

Katmai was 50 times larger than the massive 1980 eruption of Mount St. Helens in Washington state. It continued for more than two days. Glowing ash and pumice buried the nearby 40-square-mile Ukak River valley up to 700 feet deep in places; the town of Kodiak, 100 miles from the eruption, had to be evacuated. The eruption was heard 900 miles away in Ketchikan, and it dropped acid rain on Vancouver, British Columbia.

Crewmen on the steamer *Dora*, in Shelikof Strait near Kodiak when the eruption began, watched a cloud of ash overtake them until it was so dark they could not see. "Dust filled our nostrils, sifted down our backs, and smote the eye like a dash of acid," one crewman wrote. "Birds floundered, crying wildly, through space, and fell helpless on the deck." Thirty miles from the fiery mountain, a group of Natives were at their summer fishing camp. One wrote in a letter to his wife: "We are covered with ashes, in some places 10 feet and 6 feet deep. . . . We are expecting death at any moment. . . . The earth is trembling. . . ."

The Katmai eruption darkened the sky over much of the Northern Hemisphere for days, and its volcanic emissions affected world temperatures for several years. The area around the eruption was so transformed that its "lunar landscape" was used as a training ground for astronauts preparing to go to the moon.

Despite the dangers they pose, volcanic eruptions are an important part of natural renewal and recycling. They transform landscapes, create islands, and pave the way for new cycles of vegetation. Underground water heated by large bodies of molten volcanic rock, or magma, concentrates minerals such as copper, tin, gold, and silver into deposits.

© Wet Waders Inc./AlaskaStock.com ▶

MOUNT AUGUSTINE THREATENS

ONE OF ALASKA'S POTENTIALLY most dangerous volcanoes is Mount Augustine, located on its own small island only 180 miles southwest of Anchorage. The mountain erupted in 1976 and 1986 and has been seismically active since then. Augustine eruptions have produced avalanches of hot ash and gas flowing at speeds of 60 to 160 miles an hour. Researchers from the University of Alaska Fairbanks Geophysical Institute recorded temperatures of more than 1,112°F in material deposited by these flows. Scientists speculate that a fast-traveling debris flow into Cook Inlet from this island volcano could create a tsunami—an ocean wave—that would race across the inlet, threatening fishing boats and the Kenai Peninsula communities of Homer, Seldovia, Anchor Point, and English Bay (Nanwalek). ■

*The Valley of 10,000 Smokes, Katmai National Park
and Preserve, Southwestern Alaska.*

Where to See Alaska's Volcanoes

In clear weather, Cook Inlet volcanoes are visible from many parts of Anchorage and the Kenai Peninsula, especially along the Sterling Highway between Kenai and Homer.

Katmai National Park and Preserve, with its Valley of 10,000 Smokes, has at least 14 volcanoes considered active, more than in any other national park in the world. Only a few vents are still smoking, but the landscape remains spectacular.

In Sitka the beautiful Fuji-like cone of Mount Edgecumbe, now considered dormant, dominates the skyline. Intricate rock formations from flows out of Edgecumbe and nearby volcanoes are visible on the St. Lazaria Islands, a popular seabird sanctuary visited by boat tours. ◼

Mountains

I was hiking along a mountain ridge in Denali National Park and saw a group of Dall sheep. They began moving toward me, and eventually I was completely surrounded. There I sat in the middle of the flock with sweeping vistas all around me. The sheep were so close I could hear them eating.

—Bob

Nearly every part of Alaska is close to the natural wonder of mountains. With a greater variety, height, and mass than mountains anywhere else in North America, they reach to the clouds

The Arrigetch Peaks in the Brooks Range, Arctic Alaska.

and to the depths of the ocean. They surround steaming volcanoes. They stand up to ocean storms. They sift water from the moist sea air, nurturing acres of green forest and rivers of white glacial ice. They form backdrops for spectacular vistas. They influence weather as far away as the central Plains states. They call the adventurous to challenge their massive peaks and near-vertical rock faces.

Alaska has more than 30 distinct mountain ranges, but 4 large systems dominate the state:

■ The Coast Range and the St. Elias Mountains, whose highest peaks mark the southeast border between Alaska and Canada.

■ The Alaska Range, which curves through Southcentral Alaska, following the longest fault system in North America.

■ The 720-mile arc of the Brooks Range, separating arctic Alaska from the subarctic interior.

■ The 600-mile-long Aleutian Range, which extends along the Alaska Peninsula and connects westward to the volcanic mountaintops of the Aleutian Islands.

Mountains throughout Alaska exhibit vast differences in appearance and origin. Much of the Brooks Range is made of limestone formed from coral reefs that grew in an ancient tropical sea. Its granitic Arrigetch Peaks reach skyward in spectacular pinnacles with sheer faces 3,000 feet high. Most geologists consider the Brooks Range the northernmost extension of the Rocky Mountain system.

The St. Elias Mountains in Southeast Alaska and neighboring Canada are the highest coastal mountains in the world. They are

THE CHALLENGE OF DENALI

ONE OF MOUNT MCKINLEY'S most remarkable climbers was the Japanese adventurer Naomi Uemura. He climbed McKinley in August 1970 in the first solo ascent of the mountain. He returned in 1984 and completed the first winter solo climb, arriving at the summit on February 12, his forty-third birthday—then disappeared while descending. His body was never found. ■

still growing as the tectonic plates beneath them shift. The Wrangell Mountains, to their north, were formed by lava flows from ancient volcanoes.

Both ranges are part of Wrangell–St. Elias National Park and Preserve, the largest unit of the U.S. National Park system and part of a World Heritage Site that includes Glacier Bay National Park in Alaska and Tatshenshini–Alsek Provincial Park/Kluane National Park in Canada. Wrangell–St. Elias National Park contains more than half of the 16 highest peaks in the United States, including the second-tallest, Mount St. Elias (18,008 feet).

North of the Gulf of Alaska are the Chugach and Kenai Mountains. With peaks and ridges reaching to 13,000 feet, they are draped with ice fields that feed some of Alaska's most spectacular glaciers.

Alaska contains 17 of the 20 highest peaks in the United States, including the highest in North America, Mount McKinley, also known as Denali. The peak rises 20,320 feet above sea level—a dramatic 17,000 feet above its base at about 3,000 feet elevation. This may be the only mountain in the nation with two official names: Mount McKinley, according to the U.S. Geological Survey, and Denali, or "The High One," the traditional Tanana Indian name formally recognized by the State of Alaska. Mount McKinley is within Denali National Park and Preserve.

Each year more than a thousand climbers attempt to reach the summit of Mount McKinley. Less than half of them succeed, often because of temperatures that drop as low as −40°F and winds to 100 miles per hour and higher. Adding to the climbing difficulty is the fact that, because the earth's atmosphere decreases in density above 60 degrees latitude, the air on McKinley's slopes is about as thin as that of peaks up to 5,000 feet higher in the Himalayas.

Mountains in Alaska lure climbers because of their height or because they are technically challenging. A number of peaks with the most colorful names are in Southeast Alaska: Kate's Needle (10,023), Devils Thumb (9,077), Devils Paw (8,584), Rhino Peak (6,400), and the Mendenhall Towers, which rise nearly 2,500 vertical feet from the ice field below.

On the summit of Mount McKinley.

Some of Alaska's most fascinating animals live in the mountains. Dall sheep frequent alpine ridges, meadows, and steep slopes, where they can escape from predators over rugged terrain. Coastal brown bears often den at high elevations in winter and feed in alpine meadows. Some female brown bears in one part of Admiralty Island spend their entire lives in the mountains, never leaving to feed at low-elevation salmon streams. Wolverines, which require large expanses of wilderness, often take to the mountains, where they feed on carrion, small rodents, and birds. Golden eagles live primarily on birds and rodents taken from mountain slopes above treeline.

■ CONSERVATION NOTE

Loving Mountains to Death

Most mountain areas in Alaska have long been protected by their remoteness, but they are increasingly threatened by the kinds of problems created when large numbers of people flock to experience mountain landscapes. Burgeoning demands for road access, visitor facilities, helicopter tours, guided trips, and expeditions threaten fragile ecosystems and animals that, when disrupted, may have nowhere else to go.

Attempts have been made in a few areas to lessen human impacts. For example, Denali National Park has set road traffic limits. The use of private cars is limited to people who hold campground or other reservations, while additional visitors use the park's shuttle buses.

In Juneau the Mount Roberts tram whisks hundreds of tourists daily to alpine areas above town. Volunteers in the local Mountain Stewardship Program mark trails and otherwise direct people away from trampling the fragile alpine vegetation.

Where to See Alaska's Mountains

It is impossible to travel in Alaska without seeing mountains. In Southeast or Southcentral Alaska they dominate the skyline, changing character as the seasons variously promote tumbling waterfalls, verdant vegetation, fall colors, or sparkling cloaks of snow. Beneath air routes to Anchorage, the vast Wrangell, St. Elias, and Chugach Mountains unfold in a panorama of white peaks and curving glaciers that seems almost a nation in itself. Spectacular flightseeing tours around Mount McKinley are available from the town of Talkeetna.

Most Alaska highways at some point wind through mountain valleys and passes, offering expansive vistas and close-up views of rugged peaks, alpine vegetation, and precipitous drops to basins threaded by streams and rivers. Some of the most spectacular are the Richardson Highway at Thompson Pass, the Glenn Highway near Sheep Mountain, the Seward Highway, the Klondike Highway near White Pass, and the Dalton Highway around Atigun Pass. ■

Permafrost

*When I first visited Bethel, everything looked so strange
to me. Boardwalks snaked across the tundra,
connecting buildings. Utility pipes ran above ground on
elevated supports. The retaining wall along the river
was refrigerated. All because of permafrost.*

— Marge

One of Alaska's natural wonders is found underfoot. It is
permafrost, ground that remains frozen year after year. Made
up of soil and rocks as well as frozen water, permafrost forms when
the depth of winter freezing exceeds the depth of summer thawing.

*Because of permafrost, nearly half of the Trans-Alaska Pipeline
was built on elevated supports with heat-transfer fins.*

Glenn Highway showing dips in the road caused by permafrost.

Permafrost is thickest in arctic Alaska north of the Brooks Range, but it is found to some extent beneath nearly 85 percent of Alaska. On the arctic coastal plain it extends as much as 2,000 feet below the surface and is found virtually everywhere. From the Brooks Range southward its thickness gradually decreases and it becomes more and more discontinuous, broken by *taliks,* pockets of unfrozen ground. Near Anchorage, permafrost is found only in isolated patches, and in Southeast Alaska it is found only high in the mountains.

Much of the permafrost in Alaska is tens of thousands of years old. In arctic and interior Alaska, river erosion and gold mining have revealed the remains of now-extinct animals from the last great ice age 100,000 to 10,000 years ago, when animals such as woolly mammoths, mastodons, lions, and saber-toothed cats roamed what is now Alaska.

Many of the grasses, flowers, and berries of the arctic tundra owe their existence to the presence of permafrost. With only a few inches of precipitation a year, arctic Alaska could well be a barren desert. But permafrost forms a frozen floor beneath seasonally thawed ground, which can be from several inches to a few feet deep. Rainfall and snowmelt cannot percolate or drain off. Instead, water collects at the surface, providing moisture to nourish plants and forming innumerable shallow lakes and ponds. Tundra plants, in turn, insulate the permafrost beneath them from thawing. They seal out the warm temperatures and sunlight of summer so the permafrost remains frozen.

Melting of permafrost can pose problems for humans and their activities. If overlying vegetation is removed or disturbed, its insulating qualities are lost and the permafrost begins to melt. Waterlogged ground becomes soft and collapses. Buildings and roads may slump or tilt, and vehicles bog down in mud.

Alaskans have developed innovative techniques for building on permafrost so it will not melt. Houses in permafrost areas are frequently built on pilings so they will not transfer heat to the ground. Floors may be insulated. Water and sewer pipes are installed aboveground.

Engineering for the Trans-Alaska Pipeline was complicated by the fact that three-fourths of the line, which carries oil at temperatures between 82°F and 116°F, would extend across land underlain by permafrost. To prevent melting of the permafrost, more than half the pipeline was built aboveground on elevated supports, some of which are refrigerated. In places where buried pipe extends across unstable permafrost, it is wrapped with insulation, and in a few locations the pipe is insulated and buried in refrigerated ditches.

■ CONSERVATION NOTE

Is Alaska Melting?

Studies of permafrost in Alaska are providing valuable information about the potential effects of global warming. One project at the University of Alaska Fairbanks Geophysical Institute has been monitoring temperatures and depth of permafrost since 1976. Precise temperature measurements have been made in a series of holes bored 200 feet deep along a line running north to south down the middle of the state along the Trans-Alaska Pipeline.

Study results show that much of the undisturbed discontinuous permafrost south of the Yukon River has warmed significantly and some of it is thawing. That raises the possibility that roads, buildings, and other structures on thawed areas will collapse. Another problem could arise as well: As permafrost thaws it can release methane and carbon dioxide, gases that contribute to the greenhouse effect and accelerate global warming.

Where to See Alaska's Permafrost

In Northern and Interior Alaska, permafrost is frequently visible along riverbanks or road cuts. It is most obvious where large wedges or lenses of ice can be seen amid the soil. Where the Dalton Highway crosses the Yukon River, daily tourist boat trips give people a look at exposed permafrost along the riverbank.

Effects of permafrost melting can also be seen on many roads and highways in Interior Alaska. Watch for rough, wavy road surfaces and highway signs warning of "Dips."

One area recommended by Tom Osterkamp at the Geophysical Institute can be seen as you travel south on the Parks Highway from Nenana to Denali National Park. There are large depressions in the road that have been repaired repeatedly.

Buildings tilted because of melting permafrost can be seen along Farmer's Loop Road near Fairbanks. You can see aboveground water and sewer pipes in Barrow and Bethel. ■

Exposed permafrost near Atigun Pass in the Brooks Range.

Tundra

*I camped on arctic tundra at Grayling Lake for five days.
There were so many mosquitoes that every time I took the
lid off the cooking pot, a layer of dead bodies collected on
the food. A moose was virtually living in the lake to
escape the bugs. Every time I looked at it, only its nose
was visible above the water. I wished I was aquatic, too.*

—Bob

The hardiest trees can grow in much of Alaska despite extreme cold, scouring winds, and permafrost, but there comes a point at which there is not enough warmth during summer for trees to

*Porcupine caribou herd crossing the Tamayariak River
in the Arctic National Wildlife Refuge.*

complete their annual growth cycle. This point is marked by treeline, the end of the forest and, in most cases, the beginning of tundra.

Nearly half of Alaska is covered by tundra—treeless expanses of sedges, wildflowers, and dwarf shrubs such as willows and heaths. Tundra is generally grouped into three types: wet tundra, moist tundra, and alpine tundra.

In wet tundra, found on the arctic coastal plain and in parts of northwestern Alaska, the ground is saturated by standing water, and permafrost generally lies just a few inches beneath the ground's surface. Low-growing sedges lay down a thick mat of grassy vegetation, depending on extensive networks of roots and underground stems to store carbohydrates from one short growing season to the next.

On the arctic coastal plain, in areas where there are fine soils, permafrost has created tundra polygons, a kind of patterned ground that affects the nature of the plants growing on it. Tundra polygons are so common in the arctic that a special symbol is used to indicate them on topographic maps.

The polygons are formed in winter when the ground contracts from intense cold and cracks in the same patterned way that mud at the bottom of a pond or puddle does when it dries. In spring, meltwater collects in the cracks and freezes, forming vertical ice wedges that are enlarged each spring as additional meltwater flows into them and freezes. As this process is repeated over decades or centuries, the soil along the sides of the cracks is pushed up into ridges, some of which grow to be 10 to 12 inches high. This creates different habitats for plants: the center of the polygon, wet and often covered by sedges and moisture-loving mosses, and the drier ridges, where plants such as crowberry, bearberry, lichens, and dwarf willow or birch can take hold.

Moist tundra, found in the foothills and lower elevations of the Alaska Range and on many parts of the Seward and Alaska Peninsulas, is typified by cottongrass tussocks—mounds of vegetation that build up as cottongrass grows and then dies down in the same place over a number of years. Because of the cold climate, dead leaves of the 6- to 10-inch-tall plants are slow to decompose. Instead they build up into knobby mounds about the size of soccer

Alpine tundra on Douglas Island near Juneau.

———■———

balls that are infamous among human visitors trying to make their way across the landscape. Mosses and lichens grow in the moist channels between tussocks, and dwarf shrubs such as Labrador tea and arctic birch grow on drier sites. On the Aleutian Islands and the islands of the Bering Sea, moist tundra forms tall grass meadows interspersed with dense low shrubs such as cassiopes and heaths.

Alpine or dry tundra is found in barren rocky areas on mountains, bluffs, and ridgetops throughout Alaska. One of its typical plants, moss campion, grows as a ground-hugging, thick cushion less than an inch tall but sometimes a foot or more in diameter. The cushion shape helps protect the plant against the greatest hazards of its exposed location: the drying effects of wind and the scouring action of windblown sand, snow, and ice particles. The shape of the moss campion also conserves heat: Temperatures within a cushion have been found to be as much as 40 degrees warmer than the temperature of the surrounding air.

Vast numbers of mosquitoes breed in wet and moist tundra, where they pollinate tundra plants and provide food for nesting birds. Male and female mosquitoes both feed on nectar from plants, but females need the protein from blood meals—from caribou and other animals including humans—to reproduce most successfully. It has been said that the massed weight of living mosquitoes during an Alaskan summer is greater than that of all the region's caribou herds. Mosquitoes mob any available human, making insect repellent, bug jackets, and bug hats seasonal necessities in many areas.

Harassed by mosquitoes and other insects such as black flies, warble flies, and botflies, caribou seek relief by avoiding marshy areas and lake edges, facing into the wind, or standing in the open water of rivers, lakes, or the Arctic Ocean. Insect harassment is a primary cause of caribou movement during summer and may help prevent caribou overpopulation and overgrazing of the fragile tundra vegetation.

■ CONSERVATION NOTE

Shrinking Tundra

With the predicted rise in temperatures due to global warming, Alaska's tundra is expected to shrink, as parts of it are replaced by boreal forest.

In some areas of Alaska, forest expansion is limited by mountains. In Arctic Alaska, for example, the forest would have to march over the Brooks Range before it could start replacing tundra on the arctic coastal plain.

In other areas, however, there are few topographic barriers. Scientists predict that all but the highest elevations on the Seward Peninsula, which is now mostly tundra, will eventually be covered by forest. Such changes will likely affect the distribution of caribou, which depend on tundra vegetation at specific times of the year.

Where to See Alaska's Tundra

Look for wet and moist tundra throughout Northern Alaska, along much of the Bering Sea coast, and on the Alaska Peninsula. You can see extensive tundra in most of the national parklands of northern Alaska, including Gates of the Arctic National Park and Preserve, the Arctic National Wildlife Refuge, and Noatak National Preserve, and also in Denali National Park and Preserve.

Alpine tundra is found in all Alaska mountain ranges and on exposed ridges in Arctic and Southwestern Alaska. ■

© Michael DeYoung/AlaskaStock.com

Boreal Forest

We'll go back in the woods to pick blueberries with Andrew and Maggie this afternoon. For how many centuries have their people been relying on this forest to provide food, tools, shelter? Last winter at the potlatch there were songs about hunting and fishing. I wonder if there are any songs about picking blueberries?

—Marge, at Tok

M ore than 100 million acres—much of Interior Alaska—is covered by boreal, or subarctic, forest. Dominated by white and black spruce (cone-bearing evergreens), it also includes

Fall colors in the boreal forest,
Denali National Park and Preserve.

groves and stands of cold-hardy deciduous trees such as birch, aspen, and poplar, and patches of high brush, alder thickets, and wetlands. In northern parts of the forest, where trees reach the limit of their range, trees are often sparse and small—thus the Russian word for these forests, *taiga* (TYE-ga), or "little sticks."

In Alaska the boreal forest extends northward from the Kenai Peninsula to the southern slopes of the Brooks Range and westward from the Canadian border to the edge of the Yukon-Kuskokwim lowlands and the Seward Peninsula. Its northern edge marks the northern limit of treeline in Alaska.

Only a few kinds of trees can survive in this harsh environment, and their survival is often marginal. The growing season is short, temperatures commonly drop to −50 and −60°F in winter, and in many places permafrost forms an icy layer year-round only a few inches below the ground surface. Soils are cold, poorly drained, and very low in nutrients.

The hardy trees that do survive are often smaller than the same species seen farther south. A white spruce 100 to 200 years old may be only 10 to 24 inches in diameter, an average paper birch measures 8 to 9 inches in diameter, and a black spruce 100 years old may reach only 2 inches in diameter. Still, boreal trees provide Alaskans with house logs and firewood, and the forest understory is often rich in berries, mushrooms, and other wild foods.

All trees in the boreal forest have developed a way to frostproof themselves and survive at temperatures well below −40°F. Each tree has great numbers of small, empty spaces between the cells of its living tissues. When winter's cold begins to reach the cells, liquids inside them ooze out through the cell walls into the spaces, a process called extracellular freezing. Even though the liquids freeze, ice crystals do not damage the tree's living cells.

White and black spruce are well adapted to live on the cold, nutrient-poor soils of the northern forest. They do not conduct photosynthesis as efficiently as many deciduous trees, but because they keep their needles all year round, they do not need a massive burst of energy in the spring to produce new leaves. They do not lose all the nutrients within their needles, or "leaves," by dropping them in the fall. Black spruce, in fact, which occupy the poorest,

WOOD FROG

IT WEARS A DARK MASK, sounds like a miniature quacking duck, and survives extreme cold by freezing. The wood frog *(Rana sylvatica)* is found in nearly all regions of Alaska, in forest, muskeg, and tundra. It appears that the frog survives freezing in winter for the same reason that the hardiest northern trees and shrubs do—because ice crystals form in spaces between its cells, rather than within the cells where the crystals could puncture membranes and cause potentially fatal damage. ◾

least productive sites in the forest, have been found to hold their needles for as long as 25 or 30 years, while most other evergreens hold them for 8 years or less.

Because boreal trees often grow in areas underlain by permafrost, they must function with shallow roots. This often affects their stability. Seasonal freezing and thawing produce movement in the top few inches of soil, sometimes causing trees to lean haphazardly and create the appearance of a "drunken forest."

If left uninterrupted, the overall condition of the boreal forest would decline. As the trees grow, they form a closed canopy that shades the forest floor and shuts out the warmth of the sun. Because fungi and bacteria work so slowly at cold northern latitudes, fallen trees, broken branches, and dead vegetation accumulate on the forest floor. This ties up nutrients so that few are returned to the soil. This accumulated dead vegetation, and a carpet of moss that typically grows on the forest floor, insulates the ground. As the soil cools, the permafrost level rises. All these factors make the ground increasingly less suitable to support the growth of the forest.

Forest fire in the boreal forest near Tok, east-central Alaska.

But in Alaska's interior forests this declining environment is frequently modified by extensive forest fires. June thunderstorms can bring as many as 3,000 lightning strikes a day to Interior Alaska, and many of the strikes ignite forest fires. Hundreds of thousands of acres may burn in a summer, bringing not merely destruction but also a cycle of renewal that seems to be crucial to the overall health of the forest. Though fire may kill individual trees, it removes both overhanging branches and the vegetation covering the forest floor. Sunlight can reach the ground, and ash on the forest floor makes nutrients available to the opportunistic seedlings that soon spring up. Fireweed, willows, and low brush grow, followed by fast-growing quaking aspen and paper birch, and eventually white and black spruce.

Black spruce is well equipped to take advantage of this cycle. Black spruce cones may stay on the tree unopened for years, but when touched by the heat of a fire they burst open, releasing their seeds onto the forest floor, now enriched by ash and open to sunlight. One study in Alaska showed that the amount of black spruce seed released in a burned stand in a 70-day period following fire was one and a half times greater than in an adjacent unburned stand.

The boreal forest, with its changing mosaic of trees, brush patches, boggy muskegs, and shallow ponds, is home to moose, hares, lynx, squirrels, and a host of other animals. The complexity of its vegetative patches and patterns is most obvious in fall. Then, in response to declining daylight and the bite of frosty mornings, tamaracks, alders, birches, and willows send up amber and golden flares against the dark green of spruce. In the understory, blueberries, highbush cranberries, and kinnikinnik flame red in anticipation of the white mantle that will soon cover the forest.

■ CONSERVATION NOTE

Expanding Forest

At the present rate of global warming, scientists predict a worldwide rise in temperature of about 5°F within the next 80 to 100 years. In places at high northern latitudes, such as Alaska, this warming is expected to be twice as much, or about 10°F.

This amount of warming could allow the boreal forest to expand considerably as trees push their way into areas now covered by tundra. Studies over the last decade indicate that boreal forests are expanding northward at a rate of 60 miles for every 2 degrees of temperature increase. Such a change can be expected to alter the distribution of wildlife in many areas.

Where to See Alaska's Boreal Forest

The Glenn, Richardson, and Steese Highways provide some of the easiest access to the boreal forest. Rivers of the Alaskan Interior such as the Tanana, Chitina, and parts of the Yukon offer glimpses of the forest's wildlife and stages of succession. The Kobuk Valley in northwestern Alaska shows the shifting transition between forest and tundra. Around Fairbanks, the "fall sunlight" of large stands of birches in golden color is a highlight of the season. ■

Coastal Rain Forest

How much of this forest around me is water? Rain floods down from the clouds, soaks into spongy moss, hangs in the air so you can taste it. Rivers course upward through a million roots and stems, carrying water back into the sky.

—Marge

Few people associate Alaska with cool summers and relatively mild winters, but these are the norm along the coast in Southeast and Southcentral Alaska. High coastal mountains and adjacent marine waters warmed by ocean currents set the stage for

Coastal rain forest
in Southeast Alaska.

abundant snow and rainfall—an average of 100 inches a year. These conditions foster the growth of Alaska's temperate rain forest.

This coastal rain forest contains some of the greatest masses of living organisms per square foot on earth. Beneath giant western hemlock and Sitka spruce trees is a thick, luxurious carpet of moss that not only covers the forest floor but also adorns the tree trunks and surrounds their branches. Huge patches of leafy green lichens grow among the mosses, and long, draping strands of pale "old man's beard" lichens hang from tree branches. Open areas among the trees contain miniature forests of 6-foot-high devil's club and patches of blueberry thickets, ferns, and ground-hugging dwarf dogwood.

Although we marvel at the large conifers within Alaska's coastal rain forest, it is the mosses, lichens, and fungi that make these trees possible. Mosses act like giant sponges, absorbing rainwater and its dissolved nutrients and thereby preventing soil erosion, keeping tree roots moist during dry spells, and providing nutrients to the soil over extended periods of time. Lichens are able to fix nitrogen from the air and form nitrate fertilizer. Fungi attach to the tree roots and, with finely divided filaments known as hyphae (HIGH-fee), extend into surrounding soil to pick up water and essential nutrients such as phosphorus, nitrogen, potassium, and calcium, which they pass on to the host tree.

The older portions of coastal rain forest support the greatest number of deer, wolves, brown bears, bald eagles, marbled murrelets, marten, river otters, northern flying squirrels, woodpeckers, and salmon. Stands of trees older than 250 years create a mosaic of various densities, crown sizes, and interspersed openings. This allows sunlight to reach the forest floor to stimulate the growth of food plants for deer. The large branches of older trees intercept and hold snowfall in winter, allowing deer access to food when other areas are covered with deep snow. Deer, in turn, are food for wolves and brown bears, and the older trees provide the two predators with denning sites in cavities created by their massive root systems.

Most bald eagles choose large trees more than 400 years old to support their nests, which can weigh as much as a ton after years of use. Marbled murrelets nest on the moss covering the branches of older trees, where a more open crown structure allows access for these small seabirds whose wings are better designed for "flying" underwater than among trees. Marten, cat-like relatives of mink and weasels, feed on voles and mice within the older forest, and river otters den within the root wads of large, old trees.

Even dead and fallen trees are important. Northern flying squirrels, chickadees, and woodpeckers raise their young in cavities of trees that have died of old age. When trees die and fall into streams, they benefit salmon by providing protection from predators, pools for resting adults, and rearing areas for the young. As these logs decay, they also contribute important nutrients to the stream's food chain.

The forest is important to people, too. Native Tlingit and Haida peoples used wood from the forest to build plank houses, canoes, and massive totem poles, and they and other Alaskans turn to the forest today for hunting, gathering, recreation, commercial logging, and a growing tourism industry.

■ CONSERVATION NOTE

Protecting Old-Growth Rain Forest

Many coastal rain-forest mammals and birds depend on the presence of older and larger trees for food and shelter. Most of

© Mark Kelley/AlaskaStock.com ▶

SITKA SPRUCE

SITKA SPRUCE IS UNUSUAL among the spruces in that it is a coastal rather than a continental species. It is the largest of the spruces and also the largest tree within Alaska's coastal rain forest. Mature Sitka spruce grow to between 150 and 250 feet tall and 5 to 10 feet in diameter. They may live for 500 to 850 years—up to ten human lifetimes.

Sitka spruce occurs only where there is no summer drought, or where coastal fog maintains high humidity and moisture. It is a characteristic species of the perpetually wet rain-forest zone.

*In Southeast Alaska most bald eagles
nest in large, old trees.*

these large, old trees in Alaska are found in the Tongass National Forest, which covers more than 90 percent of the land area in Southeast Alaska. Although a large percentage of this area is still pristine, road building and clear-cut logging have disproportion-ately impacted valuable stands of larger trees. About 1 million acres of old-growth forest have been logged in Southeast Alaska on both public and Native-owned lands, and more than 3,000 miles of logging roads have been built.

The amount of future clear-cutting in the Tongass will be deter-mined by the U.S. Congress, which has set aside important areas from logging in the past, and by the Forest Service's Tongass Land Management Plan, which is revised every 10 to 15 years.

In the meantime, a small group of concerned citizens has been traveling about the Tongass National Forest, identifying, measuring, and mapping groves of the biggest trees. These small groves do not normally appear on the maps of forest planners and many are unprotected against timber harvest. Termed the "Landmark Tree Project," this effort has documented a series of 1-acre sites throughout the Tongass. Trees within these mapped sites often reach 200 feet tall and 6 to 9 feet in diameter.

KARST AND CAVES

LIMESTONE CAVES AND OTHER FORMATIONS of international signifi-
cance are found within the coastal rain forest of Southeast Alaska. The
type of heavily eroded landscape known as karst is produced when
acidic groundwater eats its way through limestone. Karst shows deep
shafts, crevasse-like fissures, and spires and spikes of rock at the
surface. Below ground, the acidic water has eroded caves, sinkholes,
and passages for underground streams. Some caves contain beautiful
formations—rippled, sculptured rock, mineral "icicles," and streaks of
glistening mineral deposits.

The caves provide even, year-round temperatures that have
attracted animals and people over thousands of years. Among the
remains found in caves on Prince of Wales Island are ancient human
hearths, middens, and rock paintings; otter bones as much as
8,500 years old; and remains of grizzly bears, marmots, and foxes,
none of which are found on Prince of Wales Island today.

You can see karst features at various places along the Prince of
Wales Island road system. The underground caves are very fragile.
Access to a few viewing sites under development can be arranged
through Thorne Bay Ranger Station on Prince of Wales Island. ■

Project members have found that the biggest trees usually
grow adjacent to productive salmon streams, which in turn support
bears and a variety of other wildlife. To minimize impacts on
wildlife and vegetation, the locations of many of these sites is not
being made public; however, the group hopes that a few of the big-
tree sites can be developed as ecotourism attractions on a par with
Alaska's popular tidewater glaciers, brown bears, and whales.

Where to See Alaska's Coastal Rain Forest

The best way to see the coastal forest is to walk through it
along trails from virtually any island or community in Southeast or
Southcentral Alaska. Trails near Sitka National Historic Park and
the visitor center at Glacier Bay are especially accessible. You'll
get panoramic views of the forest from ferries or tour ships, or
from sea kayaks in Prince William Sound and throughout the
Inside Passage. ■

Islands

*Even tiny, remote Alaskan islands are full of life. I love
doing biological research, so if I were ever stranded on
one of these islands, I would study black oyster-
catchers and the homing ability of limpets.*

—Bob

A laska has thousands of islands: volcanic islands still emerging
from the sea; glacier-carved islands cloaked in rain forest; rock
spires and sea stacks; grassy treeless hills clothed with wildflowers.

Islands make up nearly half the land area of Southeast Alaska.
The six largest—Prince of Wales, Chichagof, Admiralty, Baranof,

*Dutch Harbor on Unalaska Island
in the Aleutian Islands.*

© Grant Klotz/AlaskaStock.com

*Round Island, a state wildlife sanctuary in Western Alaska,
is an important haulout for walrus.*

Revillagigedo, and Kupreanof—have areas of more than 1,000 square miles each. They are entire landscapes unto themselves, with mountain peaks 3,000 to 4,000 feet high, alpine meadows, streams, lakes, estuaries, and great expanses of productive rain forest. Many of the seaways between the islands are rocky fjords carved by glaciers and later flooded by the sea. Some are as much as 2,400 feet deep, and the fjord comprising Lynn Canal and Chatham Strait is the longest in North America.

Admiralty Island, the third largest island in Southeast Alaska, includes the greatest expanse of protected old-growth temperate rain forest in the world. It is home to the world's densest population of brown bears (about 1,700 of them) and the densest nesting population of bald eagles anywhere (a nest for every mile of shoreline).

Most of Admiralty's 1,709 square miles are National Monument, and the United Nations has named the monument, in conjunction with Glacier Bay National Park, an International Biosphere Reserve.

Kodiak Island in Southwestern Alaska is the largest island in the United States, yet because of its convoluted coastline, no place on it is more than 15 miles from the sea. More than two-thirds of its 3,588 square miles is part of the 1.9-million-acre Kodiak National Wildlife Refuge. It is home to one of the largest carnivores in the world, the Kodiak brown bear, which can weigh as much as 1,400 pounds and stand 9 feet tall.

The Aleutian Islands are the westernmost and southernmost part of Alaska. They stretch 1,400 miles into the North Pacific Ocean and reach farther south than the United States/Canada border in Dixon Entrance in Southeast Alaska. The longest archipelago of small islands in the world, they have lush tundra meadows, barren volcanic peaks, and black sand beaches.

Caught where cold air from the Arctic meets warm, moist air from the south, the Aleutians have some of the worst weather in the world. Violent storms, pounding surf, and winds to 100 miles an hour are not uncommon, and fog often halts air traffic for days at a time.

Most of the Aleutians are part of the Alaska Maritime National Wildlife Refuge, which takes in some 3,000 islands, headlands, rocks, islets, spires, and reefs along the Alaskan coast. The refuge's 4.5 million acres include parcels of land from Forrester Island in Southeast Alaska to Attu Island at the tip of the Aleutians and almost to Barrow on the Arctic Ocean. About 40 million seabirds nest in the refuge, 80 percent of the total number estimated to nest in Alaska.

The Pribilof Islands, more than 275 miles off the Alaska mainland in the Bering Sea, contain some of the most valuable seabird habitat in the world in terms of abundance, diversity, and importance of species. They are home to one of the world's largest colonies of thick-billed murres, with a population of some 1.5 million birds, and 90 percent of the world's rare red-legged kittiwakes nest there. Some 1.7 million fur seals (80 percent of the world population) gather on Pribilof beaches to breed each summer.

More than 55,000 Alaskans live on islands—in small settlements or large communities such as Ketchikan, Kodiak, and Sitka. In Southeast and Southwestern Alaska, the state-funded marine highway system weaves connections among more than two dozen communities.

■ CONSERVATION NOTE

Exotic Introductions

Over centuries, island-nesting seabirds and some waterfowl have adapted to rearing their young where there are no predatory land mammals such as foxes or wolves. On many islands in Alaska this situation was drastically disrupted by the intentional or accidental introduction of animals not native to the area.

For about 100 years, between the 1830s and the 1930s, fur farming was a lucrative business in Alaska. Thousands of arctic and red foxes were released on more than 400 islands throughout the state. The foxes, which eat adult birds, their eggs, and their young, eliminated Aleutian Canada goose populations from all but three small Aleutian islands and decimated populations of seabirds, especially burrow nesters such as Cassin's and whiskered auklets, ancient murrelets, and storm-petrels.

OUTPOSTS OF SAFETY

As OUTPOSTS OF LAND surrounded by water, islands offer seabirds and some marine mammals places to breed and rest isolated from predators and close to the forage fishes they need for survival. Certain small, rocky islands provide crucial breeding habitat for Steller sea lions, whose populations are threatened in some areas of Alaska. Even a single small, rocky island can furnish a variety of nesting sites for tens of thousands of seabirds—narrow ledges for kittiwakes and murres, boulder rubble for guillemots, rock crevices for horned puffins, and soft ground in which tufted puffins and storm-petrels can excavate nest burrows. ■

Today—thanks to the voracious appetites of the foxes, which ate themselves out of house and home, to fur trappers, and to removal efforts by the U.S. Fish and Wildlife Service—foxes remain on only 32 of the 455 islands to which they are known to have been introduced. On many of these fox-free islands, large populations of seabirds have reestablished themselves. The Aleutian Canada goose has recovered enough to be reclassified from "endangered" to "threatened."

Some introduced predators have proven more difficult to eliminate. On many islands, arctic ground squirrels, voles, and house mice were introduced, sometimes by the barrelful, to feed the foxes. Norway rats have been introduced accidentally through shipwrecks and from vessels at anchor.

Where to See Alaska's Islands

Islands of the Inside Passage, Glacier Bay, and Prince William Sound provide protective waters and haulouts for sea kayakers. The Chiswell Islands near Seward, the St. Lazaria Islands near Sitka, and many others can be reached by day charters or tours. Two Aleut corporations offer guided tours of the Pribilof Islands. Lodging and guided fishing, hunting, and tours are available on Kodiak Island. ■

WATER

Oceans and Seas

In the sailboat off the coast of Coronation Island. Out
past miles of lead gray sea, a bank of white clouds
stretches across the horizon. Within minutes it's rolled
in and enveloped us. Fog! Tom has set a course of
90 degrees and we are traveling blind, ears strained for
the warning sound of surf on rocks.

—Marge

Alaska's largest natural wonder nearly surrounds the state.
Alaska is in fact a giant peninsula bordered by two oceans
and three seas. With its long Aleutian island arm flung out into the

A crab boat in the Gulf of Alaska
off Kodiak Island.

North Pacific Ocean, the state seems determined to bridge the waters between North America and Asia—and indeed it nearly does west of the Seward Peninsula, where Alaska's Little Diomede Island looks across a mere 3 miles of Bering Strait to Russia's Big Diomede Island.

The salt waters bordering Alaska are among the most productive in the world. They produce food and provide habitat for billions of fish, millions of seabirds, and over a million marine mammals. The greatest number of wild salmon in the world feed as adults in the Gulf of Alaska. They originate in fresh waters of Alaska, Japan, Russia, Canada, and all states of the U.S. Pacific Northwest.

Among seabirds, more than 50 million sooty and short-tailed shearwaters migrate up to 10,000 miles each summer from Southern Hemisphere nesting grounds to feed in Bering Sea and North Pacific waters off Alaska. Thousands of gray whales leave their winter calving grounds off Mexico to migrate some 8,700 miles each spring. They travel offshore the full length of Alaska to feed in the Bering, Chukchi, and Beaufort Seas.

The Bering Sea and the southern Chukchi Sea are especially productive because large areas of them are underlain by continental shelf, where the water is less than 650 feet deep. This is the area formerly exposed as the Bering Land Bridge when sea levels dropped as recently as 11,000 to 15,000 years ago. These relatively shallow waters are several times more productive than deep ocean waters because they fall within the range of sunlight.

Phytoplankton, tiny free-floating plants that form the base of the oceanic food chain, need sunlight to conduct photosynthesis. But they also need nutrients such as nitrogen and phosphorus, which can be carried from deep waters up over the continental shelf by a process called upwelling. The nutrients "fertilize" the phytoplankton, allowing them to conduct photosynthesis and to reproduce. This perpetuates a food chain that extends to invertebrates, fish, seabirds, polar bears, orcas, and even humans.

North of Alaska the Beaufort Sea and the Arctic Ocean are considerably less productive than the more southerly seas, partly because large areas of them are ice-covered for much of the year. But the Arctic Ocean is about 3 feet lower than the Pacific, so ocean currents flow northward and carry some nutrients and plankton from the Bering and southern Chukchi Seas into less productive northern waters.

For centuries great numbers of Alaskans have lived by and from the sea. The Aleuts of the Aleutian Islands, perhaps the most seagoing of Alaskans, developed sleek, maneuverable skin kayaks to harvest sea otters, seals, walrus, and sea lions. Coastal Yupik and Inupiat communities harvest marine mammals such as seals and sometimes whales. Commercial and subsistence fishing are mainstays of the modern economy.

Alaska typically produces about five times as much seafood as any other U.S. state, and it ranks among the top 10 seafood producers in the world. Sportfishing in salt water is both an important part of life and a source of income for many residents. Even Alaskans living far from the coast depend on salmon that are reared in the oceans.

Alaska's expanding visitor industry also relies heavily on nearby oceans and seas. More than 500,000 tourists a year (about a third of all visitors) travel to Alaska via cruise ships and state ferries, and many of Alaska's attractions—whale watching, bird watching, sea kayaking, sportfishing, and viewing tidewater glaciers—take place on or near salt water.

■ CONSERVATION NOTE

Growing Concerns

Though Alaskan waters are considered among the most pristine in the world, scientists are now beginning to find traces of

◆

ALASKA'S COASTLINE

ALASKA HAS 6,640 MILES OF COASTLINE, more than all the other 49 U.S. states combined. If the distance around islands is added, the state has 33,900 miles of shoreline, 9,000 miles more than the distance around the entire earth at the Equator. ■

▶ © Tom Soucek/AlaskaStock.com

A purse seiner takes on salmon in
Frederick Sound, Southeast Alaska.

harmful substances: acid rain, PCBs, DDT, dioxins, HCH, dibenzo-furans, chlordane, toxaphene, heavy metals, and radionucleides. Their presence is particularly problematic for Alaska's marine fish, birds, and mammals because they are generally longer lived and slower growing than those farther south and can accumulate more of these pollutants over time. Because of the cold environment, Alaskan animals also typically have more fat, the kind of tissue in which pollutants concentrate.

Coal mining and large-scale dumping of radioactive materials in regions of the former Soviet Union are of special concern, but there are other sources of pollution in high latitudes. Chemicals such as PCBs and DDT that vaporize and enter the atmosphere in warm regions can be carried northward on the winds, to condense over cold regions such as the Bering Sea and the Arctic Ocean by a process called cold-trapping.

Although pollutants in Alaskan waters have not reached levels considered harmful to humans, there is growing reason for concern. Even salmon swimming from the ocean into interior Alaska have been found to contain traces of man-made chemicals such as PCBs and DDT, and they pass them on to arctic grayling and other resident species through the freshwater food chain.

Where to See the Oceans and Seas of Alaska

Oceans and seas are perhaps Alaska's easiest natural wonder to see. Most flights to Alaska follow the coastline from the Lower 48. Thousands of visitors cruise the fjords of the Inside Passage or Prince William Sound. And the great majority of Alaska cities and tourist destinations are along the coast.

Visit Ketchikan, Wrangell, Petersburg, Sitka, Juneau, Cordova, Anchorage, Kodiak, Seward, Homer, Nome, or Barrow and you will observe the importance of marine waters to the economy, culture, and recreation of people in Alaska. ◼

© Jeff Schultz/AlaskaStock.com ▼

HIGH TIDES AND FOAMING WATER

ALASKA HAS SOME OF THE GREATEST tidal ranges in the world, with a difference of up to 33 feet between high and low tide in some parts of the state. Just south of Anchorage near the Seward Highway, such tidal ranges often create the surprising phenomenon of a bore tide: a foaming wall of water that may rise 6 feet high as it moves across Turnagain Arm.

The bore forms when an incoming tide from Cook Inlet meets the constricted entrance and shallower water of Turnagain Arm. As incoming water rises up and over water already within the arm, it rushes into the arm as a breaking wave up to 6 feet high at its leading edge. The wave is curved because the center, in the middle of the arm, travels fastest in deep water, while the sides, in shallower water, travel more slowly. The best time to see the bore is 2 hours and 15 minutes after low tide for Anchorage. ◼

Pack Ice

We've both seen pack ice near Nome and Kotzebue. It wasn't until doing research for this book that we realized how much life centers around it at various seasons: Streaming curtains of ice algae. Seals, walrus, and whales. Arctic cod. And voracious amphipods that can reduce a floating carcass to bones within hours.

—Bob and Marge

From November to May, the oceans bordering Alaska's north and northwest coasts are usually covered with pack ice. A drifting, changing mass of frozen seawater, it ranges from about

Mushing on Arctic Ocean pack ice near Barrow.

Fishing through pack ice on the Bering Sea near Kotzebue.

6 to 30 feet thick. Pack ice is not the barren wilderness we might expect. In the Bering Sea alone, it is home to about 1 million marine mammals, including seals, walrus, whales, and polar bears.

Unlike the perennial ice pack around the North Pole, the pack ice along Alaska's coasts is not solid. Floating on the moving ocean, it is a shifting mass of newly formed and forming ice, chunks of old ice broken from the polar ice pack, and floating islets and floes. Jammed together, jostled by winds and ocean currents, it drifts along the coast, where it is met by land-fast ice extending out from shore. Stresses where the moving ice pack meets land-fast ice can create ice hummocks miles long and dozens of feet high.

The pack is broken by long, narrow rifts of open water called leads (LEEDS) and pond-like areas of open water called polynyas (po-LIN-yas). Leads and polynyas may open and then refreeze. Polynyas often recur in the same locations year after year.

Most ice-loving animals follow the pack ice as it advances and recedes with the seasons. Most of them stay where leads, polynyas, or the ice edge give them easy access to open water. Herds of walrus haul out in areas of moving ice where they can rest when they are not diving to the ocean floor to feed, mostly on clams. Ringed seals prefer more solid ice close to shore. Bowhead whales follow the winter ice in the Bering Sea and rear their young on their annual migration through Bering Strait to the Arctic Ocean, where they spend the summer.

Many of these animals have special adaptations that help them live near the ice. Seals have long, heavy claws useful for digging breathing holes. Walrus have thick skulls with which they can break through ice nearly 9 inches thick. They use their tusks to maintain openings in the ice and to haul themselves up onto the drifting pack. Polar bears have rough pads on the bottom of their feet that keep them from slipping on the ice and help them run at speeds up to 25 miles per hour.

The survival of nearly all these animals may depend on tiny one-celled algae that grow on the undersurface of the ice. Able to grow at lower light levels than most other species of algae, ice algae form dense brown mats, often hanging down into the water in long, filmy strands. They attract vast swarms of small crustaceans called amphipods which may gather in colonies of nearly 1,000 individuals per square foot.

Amphipods are in turn eaten by arctic cod, the most important and abundant species of fish associated with pack ice. In contrast to other cod, the arctic cod has a mouth that angles slightly upward, enabling it to pluck algae and amphipods from the under-side of the ice.

Arctic cod are an important link in the arctic food chain, and some marine mammals, including beluga whales and ringed seals, depend on them for food. A beluga whale eats an estimated 50 pounds of cod per day. Polar bears feed mostly on ringed seals. So the survival of even large predators such as these can be traced back to ice algae.

In severe winters, pack ice has extended southward to the western tip of the Alaska Peninsula, but in mild winters it may extend only as far south as Nunivak Island. All along Alaska's north and western coast, winter ice is a hazard or barrier to shipping and navigation; yet it also can serve as a storm barrier by decreasing wind-generated waves, and it provides a platform from which people hunt, fish, travel, or conduct research on northern oceans.

We have only begun to understand the importance of pack ice to the Arctic and indeed to the world. Only recently, for example, did scientists learn where spectacled eiders, a threatened species of sea duck, spend the winter: They discovered about 400,000 eiders—nearly the entire world population—wintering in open areas in the pack ice of the Bering Sea.

■ CONSERVATION NOTE

Early Warning

Researchers are watching the ice pack closely because they consider it an early warning system that could forecast changes in the rest of the world. They believe the poles will be more severely affected by global warming than lower latitudes will be.

What they have found is not comforting. Since 1958 the average ice thickness in the Arctic Ocean has decreased 40%, and in the last decade the extent of sea ice has declined in the Arctic Ocean and the Bering Sea. Global warming is one suspected cause.

Where to See Alaska's Pack Ice

Two of the best places in Alaska to see pack ice are Barrow and Nome. In most years the Arctic Ocean near Barrow is frozen from late September or early October until mid- to late July, but northerly winds may keep or blow the ice pack against the coastline at any time.

At the Inupiat Heritage Center in Barrow, visitors can see artifacts from Mound 44, one of the most significant archaeological sites in North America. At that 500-year-old site, a sod house and the five Inupiat people inside it—two women, two adolescents, and a child—were crushed when an *ivu,* or huge raft of sea ice, rode up onto shore and buried the house. The people and most of their

BOWHEADS AND PACK ICE

BOWHEAD WHALES SPEND most of their lives in and around the ice pack. Named for their large heads and upwardly bowed mouths, they feed by using the 600 or more long strips of baleen in their mouth to sift tiny invertebrates from the sea. In spring these massive whales, which can grow to 60 feet long and weigh up to 75 tons, gather along the Bering Sea ice edge, waiting to move north to their summer feeding grounds in the Chukchi and Beaufort Seas. In fall they move south ahead of the advancing ice to winter in the central Bering Sea.

Because they must rise to the surface of the water to breathe, bowheads cannot live under solid ice, but they can navigate through cracks or leads of open water and commonly use their heads to smash breathing holes in ice 9 to 10 inches thick. Pads of fibrous tissue on the top of the whale's head soften the impact of the blows.

If the whales cannot break through the ice, they may simply lift the flexible sea ice with their backs, breathe through the cracks created, then let the ice down and continue on their way. Migrating bowheads often leave a trail of telltale openings or hummocks where they have lifted or broken the ice during their passage. ◼

possessions were preserved in the frozen ground until they were excavated in the early 1980s.

Pack ice usually covers the Bering Sea near Nome from mid-November until late May. On the third Saturday in March, the Nome Lions Club sponsors the Bering Sea Ice Golf Classic, a 6-hole course played on the frozen Bering Sea. From late March till the ice goes out in May, it's possible to see ice algae, amphipods, and seals. Bowhead and gray whales are usually seen migrating northward in late May and early June.

In Native cultural centers and museums throughout Alaska, visitors can see traditional tools, clothing, and artifacts that reflect the Yupik, Aleut, and Inupiat people's complex and successful adaptations to hunting sea mammals in the ice pack. ◼

Rivers and Lakes

Spring breakup on the Yukon! Millions of ice chunks
swirl in the current, crash together, and pile up into
gigantic mounds. But even more impressive are the
sounds—crackings, thundering, and a deep underlying
hiss as the ice rips free of its winter bonds.

—Marge, at Fort Yukon

Alaska has more than 12,000 rivers, including 7 of the
20 largest in the United States. Along with uncounted
smaller streams and creeks, they produce more than one-third of
the nation's entire average annual stream outflow.

Trail Lakes on the Kenai Peninsula,
Southcentral Alaska.

While most rivers in the United States have been regulated or influenced by humans, all major Alaskan rivers are free-flowing. Only a few small streams have been harnessed for hydroelectric power, and a diversion dam on the Chena River near Fairbanks is the only large-scale flood-control project in the state.

The Yukon, Alaska's largest river by far, is the third longest river in the United States and the fifth largest in terms of stream flow. After a 580-mile start in Canada, it flows for 1,400 miles across central Alaska in a great meandering arc. The Yukon and its tributaries drain a third of the state's land area, dramatically influencing landscape, vegetation, wildlife, and human history.

Nearly all major Alaskan rivers, including the Yukon, are influenced by meltwater from glaciers. Four major rivers—the Kuskokwim, the Tanana, the Susitna, and the Copper—begin at glaciers, and so do many other streams. Glacial streams are characterized by milky water filled with sediment, or glacial "flour." Their flows vary considerably, with peaks in midsummer and often dramatic increases from morning to night. Hikers in the backcountry of Denali National Park, for example, need to plan stream crossings early in the morning before the water rises.

Permafrost also affects many Alaska rivers. Arctic rivers carry a larger percentage of the precipitation that falls on their watersheds than temperate rivers do. That's because permafrost prevents surface water from draining through the frozen soil.

Virtually all Alaska rivers freeze at least partially during winter. On the North Slope, streams freeze solid for as much as seven months of the year, except for spring-fed portions of some of the major rivers. The Yukon usually freezes over from late October or early November until early or mid-May.

Spring breakup of river ice is a major event in most interior Alaska villages, where April and May bring an annual threat of flooding from ice jams. One of the premier spring events in Alaska is the Nenana Ice Classic, in which thousands of people attempt to win cash prizes by guessing the precise minute of ice breakup on the Tanana River.

Many Alaska rivers are pristine. They flow through beautiful wilderness areas and create spectacular landscapes by erosion.

Twenty-five of them are classified under the Wild and Scenic Rivers Act. Including designated tributaries, Wild and Scenic Rivers in Alaska total 3,210 miles—much more than in any other state and 29 percent of the nation's total. The Noatak River, which heads in Gates of the Arctic National Park, is the centerpiece of the largest untouched river basin in the United States. The Noatak drainage is internationally recognized by the United Nations as a Biosphere Reserve.

In Alaska, where much of the landscape is rugged and sparsely populated, rivers are indispensable as transportation corridors. Alaskans travel the rivers by boat in summer and by snow machine and other vehicles in winter. Nearly all inland villages, including more than 65 communities on the Yukon, Koyukuk, Kobuk, and Kuskokwim Rivers, are located on major rivers or their tributaries because rivers provide both transportation and fish for food.

Alaska has some 3 million lakes more than 20 acres in size. Iliamna Lake, with an area of 654,000 acres, is Alaska's largest. It also produces more sockeye salmon than any other lake in the world, contributing immensely to Alaska's Bristol Bay salmon fishery.

Some unusual types of lakes are found in Alaska, such as thaw lakes on the North Slope, which form over permafrost and tend to be oriented in parallel rows because of prevailing wind action, and glacial lakes filled with icebergs at the faces of many glaciers.

Bering Land Bridge National Preserve has four of the bodies of water known as *maar* lakes. These crater-type lakes were formed when volcanic magma rose from the earth, met groundwater and permafrost, and caused massive steam explosions. Devil Mountain Lake, the largest of the lakes, has an unusual double crater. These four maar lakes are the largest of their type on earth.

Glacier movements have at times formed and violently drained large lakes, as when Hubbard Glacier near Yakutat dammed Russell Fiord in 1986 and formed a lake 30 miles long and 2 miles wide. A few months later the glacier ruptured, and the lake roared free at a rate of nearly 3.7 million cubic feet per second. The event was the largest lake-outburst discharge ever recorded.

© Jim Wark/AlaskaStock.com

*Rivers flowing through the Nutzotin Mountains in
Wrangell–St. Elias National Park.*

THE GIFTS OF SALMON

THE ALASKA DEPARTMENT OF FISH AND GAME has identified some 13,000 Alaskan streams and 2,000 lakes that support runs of salmon, and there are probably many more. They produce some of the largest wild salmon runs in the world. In 1997, 123 million salmon were taken in Alaska commercially. Sport anglers, both residents and visitors, harvested about 1.1 million salmon. Another 1.3 million were taken for subsistence.

Salmon contribute benefits to ecosystems of many types. Studies indicate that some 14 species of mammals, 23 species of birds, and numerous fish are dependent or nearly dependent on salmon carcasses, young, or eggs for food. Without salmon, Alaska would have greatly decreased numbers of bears, sea lions, river otters, bald eagles, mergansers, kingfishers, and arctic char.

Recent studies have traced isotopes of nitrogen and carbon, two important nutrients, from dead salmon into the ecosystems along rivers. They found that salmon provided 18 percent of the nitrogen in streamside trees, 25 to 30 percent of the nitrogen and carbon found in insects, and 25 to 40 percent of the nitrogen and carbon in young salmon, which feed on the insects. ■

Alaska lakes take much of their drama from spectacular surrounding scenery and superb fishing. Like rivers, they serve as transportation routes and often provide access to remote areas by floatplane in summer and ski plane or snow machine in winter. The number of pilots per capita in Alaska is six times the national average, and many of them fly floatplanes that land on lakes, rivers, and salt waters.

■ CONSERVATION NOTE

Pioneers

While environmental problems are driving wild salmon runs to extinction in the Pacific Northwest, new salmon runs are being created naturally in Alaska as glaciers retreat. In Glacier Bay, for example, scientists estimate that more than 300 new streams have been formed within the last 200 years. About 60 percent of them are now believed to have salmon runs.

A number of lakes created by retreating glaciers have also been colonized by salmon. In Kenai Fjords, Upper Delusion Lake, which only began to form in the mid-1970s, supported a run of almost 1,000 sockeye salmon by 1997.

Where to See Alaska's Rivers and Lakes

A number of Alaskan rivers, streams, and lakes can be reached by road. A count of listings in *The MILEPOST*, a guide to Alaska's highways, tallied 637 access points for streams and 319 for lakes. Riverboat excursions leave daily in summer on the Stikine River near Wrangell, the Tanana near Fairbanks, and the Yukon near Eagle. Fly-in trips are available to fishing lodges or public recreational cabins, and bear-watching tours can be arranged at McNeil River on the Alaska Peninsula, at Brooks Falls in Katmai National Park and Preserve, and at Pack Creek near Juneau.

Lakes and portions of two rivers in Kenai National Wildlife Refuge combine to form the only nationally designated canoe trails in the Alaska refuge system: the 80-mile Swanson River trail (connecting more than 40 lakes plus 46 miles of the Swanson River) and the 60-mile Swan Lake trail (connecting 30 lakes with forks of the Moose River). Wood-Tikchik State Park near Dillingham contains two separate systems, each with six large, interconnected lakes, and Katmai National Park has a circular route nearly 100 miles long for canoeists and kayakers.

You can take river rafting and wilderness float trips on many of Alaska's rivers, including the Kobuk, the Yukon, the Tatshenshini, and six rivers in Gates of the Arctic National Park. ■

Wetlands

*I saw thousands of shorebirds. They formed a dark
mass at least 50 feet wide as far as I could see along the
water's edge. Sometimes a flock would feed right at my
feet, and I could hear them talking.*

—Bob, at Copper River Delta

Alaska has between 170 million and 200 million acres of
wetlands, more than two-thirds of all wetlands in the United
States. These wetlands include landscapes where water is the
dominant influence, such as freshwater and saltwater marshes,
muskegs, bogs, mudflats, and wet tundra.

*Wetlands and cottongrass on
the arctic coastal plain.*

Many wetlands in Alaska are unique because they cover large expanses of land that have not been altered by agricultural or industrial development. They foster aquatic plants and invertebrates, waterfowl and shorebirds, small rodents, raptors, and mammals such as beavers, muskrats, and moose. Lit by the Far North's long summer daylight, they provide places where animals can feed for more hours per day than at lower latitudes.

With wetlands disappearing worldwide at a rapid rate, Alaska's vast wetlands have become increasingly important to entire populations of birds from many parts of the hemisphere. A significant percentage of North America's waterfowl—some 10 million swans, geese, and ducks—nest in Alaska wetlands each year. Banding studies have shown that, after nesting, waterfowl from Alaska travel to all the other U.S. states, most Canadian provinces, Mexico, and as far south as Panama.

Alaska's wetlands also feed and protect waterfowl that nest in other countries. Snow geese from Canada come to feed in the wetlands of the Arctic National Wildlife Refuge each fall. All brant from Canada and Russia intermingle with those from Alaska and spend six to nine weeks each fall on Izembek Lagoon and nearby areas around Cold Bay on the Alaska Peninsula. The birds feed on eelgrass from one of the largest eelgrass beds in the world to prepare for a 3,000-mile nonstop fall migration to California or Mexico.

Three other Alaska wetlands are of particular importance to birds:

■ The Yukon-Kuskokwim Delta in Western Alaska, one of the largest river deltas in the world, provides nesting habitat for millions of waterfowl and shorebirds.

■ The Yukon Flats north of Fairbanks supports one of the highest densities of nesting ducks in North America.

■ The Copper River Delta in Southcentral Alaska provides a rest and refueling stop for shorebirds migrating each spring to Western and Northern Alaska, Siberia, and Canada.

Aside from their value to bird populations, Alaska wetlands are valuable beyond measure for other purposes. They provide sheltered areas where young salmon can grow rapidly before leaving to cope with the rigors of the ocean. Except where

Wetlands near Valdez, Southcentral Alaska.

continuous permafrost is present, they spread water from rivers and streams over broad areas, allowing it to percolate gradually into underwater aquifers. Wetlands help precipitate out solids and, by subjecting them to the action of microbes in the mud, aid in removing toxic substances. They provide nutrients to the oceans and seas with which they are often connected.

Undeveloped wetlands are among the most productive environments in the world, and many Alaskans depend on them for subsistence and recreation. People harvest fish, waterfowl, large mammals, berries, and various plants from these important areas.

■ CONSERVATION NOTE

Draining Earth and Sky

Wetlands have been lost at an alarming rate throughout most of the United States, and with them is lost crucial wintering and feeding habitat for waterfowl and shorebirds. In California alone, where a major portion of the waterfowl that nest in Alaska spend the winter, 91 percent of wetlands have already given way to development and agriculture.

In his beautiful and inspiring book *Tracks in the Sky,* Peter Steinhart writes about the loss of wetlands along the Pacific Flyway. "We are slowly strangling the flyway," he writes. "One day, we may look out over an endless plain of concrete and asphalt and glass and find that we have drained the skies."

Alaska has the lowest rate of wetland loss per state, but specific localities, particularly around urban areas, have sustained significant losses. As the state's population increases and human activities become more pervasive, those losses are sure to increase.

Where to See Alaska's Wetlands

There are innumerable tideflats, estuaries, muskegs, and other wetlands near Alaska roads, trails, and communities. Some of the most accessible, which offer good viewing of waterfowl and shorebirds, are Mendenhall Wetlands State Game Refuge in Juneau, Potter Point State Game Refuge in Anchorage, Creamer's Field Migratory Waterfowl Refuge in Fairbanks, and the Copper River Delta near Cordova. ■

◄ © Chris Arend/AlaskaStock.com

Glaciers

When I moved to Juneau in 1960, Mendenhall Glacier was
a solid mass of ice on the far side of the lake. Now that it
has retreated, it has exposed a large area of glacially carved
rock. The rock is covered with purple mountain saxifrage,
nesting gulls, and terns. It is a wonderful place to explore.

—Bob

Nearly 30,000 square miles—about 5 percent of Alaska—are
covered by glaciers. Among them are:

Old glaciers. Harding Glacier, on the Kenai Peninsula, dates
back 10,000 years to the Ice Age.

Hubbard Glacier calving in Russell Fiord
Wilderness Area near Yakutat.

70

New glaciers. Two glaciers have formed in the Mount Katmai caldera since the massive volcanic eruption of 1912.

Galloping glaciers. Variegated Glacier near Yakutat surges forward every 15 to 20 years. During 1982-83 it advanced as much as 203 feet a day.

Retreating glaciers. Portage Glacier south of Anchorage, Alaska's most-visited glacier, has been retreating an average of 300 feet per year for the last 5 years. It is no longer visible from the Forest Service visitors center.

Backyard glaciers. Mendenhall Glacier in Juneau is a mere 1.2 miles from one of the city's large residential areas.

Roadside glaciers. Matanuska Glacier is accessible from several points along the Glenn Highway.

Waterfront glaciers. There are 20 active tidewater glaciers in Prince William Sound and 10 in Johns Hopkins Inlet, a single part of Glacier Bay.

Hanging glaciers. Explorer Glacier on the road to Portage Glacier sits high on a valley wall and doesn't reach to the valley floor.

Dying glaciers. Parts of Muldrow Glacier in Denali National Park have not moved in so long that brush and trees are growing on its surface.

Unnamed glaciers. Nearly 100,000 of them.

Alaska is also home to the largest glacier in North America (Bering Glacier near Cordova), the southernmost active tidewater glacier in the Northern Hemisphere (Le Conte Glacier near Petersburg), and the deepest and thickest temperate glacier yet measured in the world (Taku Glacier south of Juneau, which was measured at 4,845 feet thick).

Most glaciers in Alaska are "warm" glaciers—that is, their temperatures vary little from the surface to the bottom, and they are not frozen to the rocks beneath them. A few glaciers in the Brooks Range are "cold" glaciers. Their temperatures get colder with the depth of ice, and they are frozen to the rock beneath them.

Glaciers are found in Alaska not where the weather is coldest but where there is the greatest precipitation. In Southeast and Southcentral Alaska, prevailing winds push warm, moist air from the Pacific Ocean toward high coastal mountains. As the air meets

Hikers on Riggs Glacier in Glacier Bay National Park and Preserve.

the mountains and is forced upward, it cools and drops up to 300 inches of precipitation a year, much of it at high, cold altitudes. Accumulating year after year faster than it melts, the snow compacts, forming extensive ice fields and glaciers.

Steep terrain in Southeast and Southcentral Alaska makes Alaska glaciers particularly active and fast-moving. In the case of tidewater glaciers, which terminate in salt water, moderate sea level temperatures increase cracking, melting, and calving, during which gigantic chunks of ice break off from the glacier's face.

Animals gather in great numbers in front of some Alaska tidewater glaciers. Glacier Bay's largest breeding colony of black-legged kittiwakes, for example, nests on exposed rocky cliffs adjacent to Marjorie Glacier. There the gulls rear their young with little disturbance from land-based predators, and they feed on the abundant invertebrates attracted to the nutrient-rich water at the face of the glacier. Ice calving off the face of the glacier makes the location even more attractive: It causes upwellings in the water, bringing invertebrates to the surface where the kittiwakes can easily reach them.

Harbor seals gather on floating icebergs in front of active tidewater glaciers, and they often create a loud cacophony to the accompaniment of waves and calving ice. The largest concentration of harbor seals in Alaska is found in Glacier Bay, where an estimated 3,000 to 5,000 seals live in Johns Hopkins Inlet. Icebergs at the face of glaciers provide safety from predators such as bears and wolves, and from killer whales (orcas), the seals' main predator, which seem to avoid these ice-choked fjords.

THE BERING LAND BRIDGE

DURING THE LAST WORLDWIDE GLACIAL ADVANCE between 25,000 and 11,000 years ago, so much of the world's water was hoarded in glaciers that the sea level dropped as much as 400 feet. Part of the Bering Sea floor emerged as dry land, forming a land bridge that connected the continents of Asia and North America. Later, as the tremendous glaciers melted, water flooded back into the sea, and now the continents are separated by a shallow ocean.

The land bridge was actually a broad plateau as much as 1,000 miles wide. Plants, animals, and eventually early peoples moved across it. In 1980 the Bering Land Bridge National Preserve was established to protect the natural and human history of this region. The preserve is close to Bering Strait, which today separates the Alaskan and Russian mainlands by a mere 55 miles. ■

Many Alaska glaciers are fed by ice fields, vast areas where snow and ice build up and large glaciers interconnect. Bagley Icefield near Cordova, which includes the massive Bering Glacier, is the largest and longest in North America. It is 126 miles long and covers more than 1,900 square miles. Harding Icefield in the Kenai Mountains feeds 36 named glaciers and covers 1,145 square miles. It receives more than 30 feet of snow a year. Juneau Icefield, which covers more than 1,200 square miles in Alaska and extends into British Columbia, receives more than 100 feet of snow a year.

■ CONSERVATION NOTE

Will Sea Level Rise?

Glaciers store tremendous amounts of fresh water. Alaska glaciers and ice fields contain nearly three times as much water as do all the state's millions of rivers, streams, ponds, and lakes. Scientists who predict that global warming will cause sea levels to rise worldwide estimate that glacier melt will contribute about one-third of the rise. The melting of polar ice sheets and thermal expansion of seawater will contribute the other two-thirds.

Some scientists, however, predict that Alaska's glaciers may not contribute all that much. They say that as the climate in Alaska warms, snowfall will increase at higher elevations, and the state's glaciers will actually grow—at least up to an annual average warming of about 8 degrees Fahrenheit.

Where to See Alaska's Glaciers

It would be difficult to travel in Southeast or Southcentral Alaska without encountering glaciers. You can drive to them, see them from a cruise ship, fly over them, hike beside them, kayak in front of them, even walk or ride a dogsled on them.

Mendenhall Glacier in Juneau and Portage Glacier near Anchorage are two of Alaska's top 10 visitor attractions. Glaciers are prominent features of Glacier Bay and Kenai Fjords National Parks, Prince William Sound, Denali National Park, and Tracy Arm south of Juneau. ■

Hot and Cold Springs

*When I was studying Dolly Varden char at Hood Bay
Creek on Admiralty Island, I noted large schools of
young fish moving upstream in the late fall. Later I
found them living in spring areas near the creek's
headwaters. Apparently they needed the springs in
order to survive the winter.*

—Bob

Volcanic activity set the stage for the formation of hot springs
throughout Alaska. A few springs in the volcanically active
Aleutian Islands and Wrangell Mountains are heated by magma,

*Outdoor pool at Chena Hot Springs Resort,
Interior Alaska.*

the molten rock found deep beneath the earth's crust and at times extruded through volcanoes. But most hot springs in Alaska are created by groundwater migrating through rocks associated with old magma chambers—granitic rocks that have solidified.

Rocks associated with these old chambers can remain hot for hundreds of thousands of years. Groundwater traveling through them via fractures and faults becomes heated and, when discharged to the surface, produces hot springs. These springs are long-lived and reliable because granite is hard and relatively insoluble, so the fractures remain open for a long time. Additional heat is also transferred to rocks, and ultimately to the spring water, from the decay of radioactive isotopes such as thorium, uranium, and potassium commonly associated with granite.

Alaska has at least 121 hot springs, many with surface temperatures ranging from 100°F to 160°F. About half of the springs are found along the Aleutian volcanic arc. The others are scattered throughout the state. About a dozen have been developed for public use, and many have been used by local people for generations.

Although people enjoy soaking and relaxing in hot springs, freshwater and seagoing fish in many parts of Alaska depend on cold springs for their very survival. Cold springs generally maintain a temperature around 40°F year-round—and thus they are able to keep certain portions of arctic rivers and streams open while most fresh water freezes for the 7- to 8-month-long winter. Scientists estimate that during an arctic winter the amount of freshwater available to fish, even within larger rivers, may be as little as 1 to 5 percent of the summer flow. In these relatively small areas of open water, entire populations of arctic grayling and Dolly Varden, including fish of all age groups, may gather until the rivers open again in spring.

Cold springs occur in northern Alaska because water absorbs heat from the sun in summer and stores it. Some of the heat is transferred to the ground through the beds of lakes and streams, thus often maintaining the patches and corridors of unfrozen ground called *taliks* beneath the water bodies, which in many cases are surrounded by the perennially frozen ground of

*Cold springs keep sections of the Chilkat River from freezing,
Chilkat Bald Eagle Preserve, Southeast Alaska.*

continuous permafrost. Taliks connect arctic rivers to flowing groundwater, allowing for the upwelling of springs that keep portions of the rivers above freezing temperature.

Fish also benefit from cold springs in other parts of Alaska. Spring-fed portions of rivers are usually the most reliable places for salmon to spawn. Springs help keep parts of glacial rivers free from silt. They help provide more consistent year-round flows of water. And in winter they provide ice-free areas for fish eggs and young.

The way cold springs can benefit fish and other animals is readily apparent along a 3- to 5-mile stretch of the Chilkat River north of Haines in Southeast Alaska. In this area, sand and gravel have accumulated several hundred feet thick on the glaciated valley bottom, and they are saturated with water that maintains a temperature of about 40°F. When water from this aquifer wells up in the river, it is warm enough to keep portions of the river from freezing in winter. This provides ideal spawning habitat for a late run of up to half a million chum salmon beginning in October. The

Bailey Bay Hot Springs, north of Ketchikan in Southeast Alaska.

salmon carcasses and eggs in turn provide bountiful food for bald eagles, mergansers, gulls, and ravens at a time when food is in short supply elsewhere.

Every year up to 3,600 bald eagles—the largest concentration of eagles in the world—gather in this valley during October and November, and many stay through February. Recognizing the importance of this phenomenon and the surrounding river and valley, the Alaska legislature in 1982 established the 48,000-acre Alaska Chilkat Bald Eagle Preserve, a unit like no other within the state park system. The preserve has become a focal point for visitors from all over the world—all, it could be said, because of the existence of the cold springs that well up into the river.

■ CONSERVATION NOTE

An Alternative Energy Source?

A number of countries have devised successful ways to harness the energy found in hot springs and other geothermal sources. In Alaska geothermal energy has so far been used only to heat small buildings and sometimes support small-scale agriculture at places like Chena, Circle, Manley, and Bell Island Hot Springs.

In 1980 the U.S. Geological Survey estimated that 1,031 quads of geothermal energy could be accessible in Alaska. That is an amount equivalent to 134 billion barrels of oil—more than 10 times the total production from Alaskan oil fields between 1978 and 1998.

Also in 1980, the Alaska Division of Geological and Geophysical Surveys and the Alaska Division of Energy and Power Development recommended more than a dozen hydrothermal sites for potential development. Geothermal sites such as these may be explored as yet one more source for alternative energy in addition to wind, sun, and low-impact hydropower.

Where to See Alaska's Hot Springs

Among the hot springs in Alaska available for public use are:

Baranof Warm Springs, 20 miles east of Sitka on the east coast of Baranof Island.

Bell Island Hot Springs, a fishing camp and resort north of Ketchikan.

Chena Hot Springs, 56 miles east of Fairbanks via the Chena Hot Springs Road.

Chief Shakes Hot Springs, 12 miles up the Stikine River and 22 miles from Wrangell.

Circle Hot Springs, 136 miles northeast of Fairbanks via the Steese Highway.

Goddard Hot Springs, 16 miles south of Sitka on the west coast of Baranof Island.

Manley Hot Springs, 152 miles west of Fairbanks via the Elliott Highway.

Pilgrim Hot Springs, 8 miles down a gravel road off the Nome-Taylor Road.

Serpentine Hot Springs, in the Bering Land Bridge National Preserve, accessible by plane from Nome and Kotzebue.

Tenakee Springs, in the community of the same name on Chichagof Island, 50 miles northeast of Sitka.

White Sulphur Springs, 65 miles northwest of Sitka on Chichagof Island. ■

S K Y

Aurora Borealis

*Nearly midnight. Tom called me out to see the Northern
Lights. They are pale green and white. Swirling and
racing across the sky, they are a vibrant, pulsating
dome over the snow-covered mountains and trees.*

—Marge

The dancing displays of the aurora borealis, or Northern Lights,
are highlights of the Alaskan winter. Auroras are often seen
as great arcs, bands, or spirals of greenish white light stretching
across the night sky. Some pulsate in brightness while others
flicker on and off. Some look like waving curtains partially edged

*The aurora swirls above a cabin
in Southcentral Alaska.*

in crimson red, or veils of light, or bundles of near-vertical rays that ripple and twist and sometimes race across the sky.

Auroras begin with gigantic explosions on the sun that send streams of charged particles—mostly electrons and protons—hurtling toward Earth at 2 million miles per hour. Some of the particles enter the earth's magnetic field, where they are accelerated to about 134 million miles per hour and are driven down into the atmosphere in the polar regions. Between about 240 and 70 miles above the earth's surface, they collide with molecules and atoms of gases, mostly oxygen and nitrogen, in the atmosphere. These collisions release energy in the form of heat and light—and if enough collisions occur, we see them as the aurora.

Auroral activity is always present at some level in the upper atmosphere, but it isn't bright enough to be seen in daylight or during Alaska's bright summer nights. During dark, clear nights, however, and especially when there is intense solar activity, we get to see this natural light show of the northern world. Auroral displays are said to be brighter over northern Alaska and eastern Siberia than anywhere else in the world.

Over the course of an evening the aurora follows a typical pattern, often beginning with a diffuse glow to the northern sky, changing to a gentle arc, then moving like a curtain blown by a breeze. It is usually most intense between midnight and about 2:00 A.M., when it may fold, twist, and dance or swirl across the sky. The movement, of course, is an illusion, created as lights from

FORECASTING THE AURORA

SCIENTISTS AT THE UNIVERSITY OF ALASKA FAIRBANKS Geophysical Institute and the Poker Flat Research Range collaborate to predict the intensity of upcoming auroras on a weekly basis. They gather information about the earth's magnetic field from a worldwide network of instruments accessible through the Internet, then combine that with data from previous solar rotations to come up with an aurora forecast that is carried on the institute's Web site (www.gi.alaska.edu). ■

atomic collisions flash on and off in a sequence that creates the appearance of motion.

An auroral arc can be as much as 1,000 miles long east to west, but its thickness north to south may be only about a mile. How it appears to us depends on our vantage point, and the colors we see depend on the types of atmospheric gas involved in collisions and the density of the atmosphere where collisions take place.

Most auroras are greenish white and are produced by collisions with atomic oxygen in the upper atmosphere. Crimson red, sometimes fringing the lower edge of an auroral curtain, is produced by collisions involving molecular nitrogen. Rare blue and purplish auroras are caused by energy spanning a large vertical range of the ionosphere and exposed to sunlight or bright moonlight.

The energy released by the aurora can cause problems, especially during periods of intense activity called auroral storms.

CAN WE HEAR THE AURORA?

THERE ARE NUMEROUS DOCUMENTED REPORTS of people hearing auroras in Alaska and elsewhere. Most describe the sound as a hissing, swishing, whooshing, or crackling. Scientists at the University of Alaska Fairbanks Geophysical Institute have analyzed the reports and concluded that sounds associated with the aurora are a real physiological phenomenon. But no one can prove the sounds are made by the aurora, and no recordings have ever been produced.

We cannot hear the aurora directly, according to the Geophysical Institute, because it occurs from high above the earth in the thin air of the ionosphere where sound waves do not carry. It is known that electrical currents are induced on the ground during auroral storms. Perhaps, as some scientists think, this creates an electrical discharge from nearby objects such as trees or buildings and causes the hissing-like sounds that many people hear.

The institute has produced a video, *The Aurora Explained*, available through Geophysical Institute, University of Alaska Fairbanks, 903 Koyukuk Drive, Fairbanks, AK 99775; phone (907) 474-7487. ■

A brilliant aurora shares the sky with the Big Dipper.

This energy can induce current in long conductors near the earth's surface, such as telephone lines or pipelines. Intense auroral activity has caused power outages and disrupted TV and radio reception. In January 1997 it incapacitated a $200 million communication satellite, and it is blamed for causing corrosion in the Trans-Alaska Pipeline. There's also evidence that it can affect weather and the migration of birds.

Where to See Alaska's Aurora Borealis

Spectacular auroral displays can be seen in many parts of Alaska, but they are visible most frequently north of the Alaska Range. When nights are dark and skies are clear, the Fairbanks area is an excellent and reliable place to see auroras. Places farther north, such as Circle, are more difficult to get to, but they are better yet. The best time to look for auroras in Alaska is from about mid-August to mid-April and between about 10:00 P.M. and 3:00 A.M.

Auroras seen by people traveling over Alaska by jet on dark nights appear twice as bright as those seen from the ground. Here are some hints to enhance viewing, based on Alaskan Neil Davis's *Aurora Watcher's Handbook:* If you are traveling north, sit on the right side of the jet. If you're southbound sit on the left. To eliminate the reflection of cabin lights in the window, try holding a blanket or coat up behind your head as a shield. ◼

Midnight Sun

I helped a graduate student conduct a study of arctic grayling at a lake about 220 miles north of Fairbanks. We lived in a small mountain tent. There was no shade. The sun shone day and night. The temperature was about 80°. I longed for darkness.

—Bob

Sunshine at midnight. Twenty-four-hour daylight. Alaska receives more sunlight in spring and summer than any other state and many other parts of the world. In Barrow, the state's northernmost community, the sun does not set for more than two

*Moose feeding under the midnight sun,
Wonder Lake, Denali National Park and Preserve.*

and a half months—from May 10 until August 2. (The downside of this phenomenon in Barrow is that from November 18 until January 24, the sun never rises above the horizon.)

The real boundary of the midnight sun is the Arctic Circle, latitude 66 degrees 33 minutes north. That imaginary line marks the lowest latitude at which the sun remains above the horizon for a full 24 hours during summer solstice (June 20 or 21) and below the horizon for a full 24 hours during winter solstice (December 21 or 22).

Nearly one-third of Alaska lies above the Arctic Circle, but Alaskans are fairly informal about claiming they live with the midnight sun. All parts of the state enjoy long daylight hours in summer, even Ketchikan, the state's southernmost population center, where there are more than 17 hours of daylight on June days.

◆

QUALITIES OF NORTHERN LIGHT

MANY PEOPLE WHO VISIT or live in Alaska notice special qualities to the light. Some say it seems muted compared with the harsh daylight of more southerly locations. Some say shades of yellow are scarce or missing from the color spectrum in winter daylight.

Art professor and painter Kes Woodward at the University of Alaska Fairbanks writes that "the thing that makes the light in Alaska so extraordinary, so magical—not just for artists but for all of us, I think—is the shallow angle of the sun at this latitude. It gives us a lot longer twilight, not just in summer but in winter, too."

Woodward cites a description in artist Rockwell Kent's book *Wilderness: A Journal of Quiet Adventure in Alaska*. Kent wrote from Resurrection Bay near Seward, where he spent the winter of 1918–19 in an isolated cabin with his son:

> Ah, the evenings are beautiful here and the early
> mornings, when the days are fair! No sudden springing
> of the sun into the sky and out again at night; but so
> gradual, so circuitous a coming and a going that nearly
> the whole day is twilight, and the quiet rose color morning
> and evening seems almost to meet the noon. ■

Long daylight hours benefit Alaska's plants because plants generally begin making food through photosynthesis as soon as the sun rises, and they continue until sunset. Warmth from the sun also helps, until temperatures reach into the high 80s, which is not uncommon in Interior Alaska. Then photosynthesis actually decreases.

Parts of Alaska such as the Tanana Valley between Fairbanks and Delta and the Matanuska Valley near Anchorage are famous for their production of gigantic vegetables. Among the largest vegetables have been a 98-pound cabbage from Wasilla, an 18.9-pound carrot from Palmer, and a 347-pound pumpkin from Homer on the Kenai Peninsula.

Studies have shown some interesting effects of midnight sun on plants in Alaska. In 1960 a forester measured seasonal growth of white spruce in Interior Alaska at the same times that another forester measured growth of white spruce in Massachusetts. Over the course of the year, the studies showed that trees at both locations produced the same amount of wood. The Alaskan trees just did it in half the time required by those in Massachusetts.

Alaska is famous, or infamous, for its biting insects, including mosquitoes, black flies, and no-see-ums. The abundance of standing water provides breeding habitats, but long daylight hours also benefit insects a great deal. When the sun shines for most of the day, the ground stays constantly warm rather than cooling at night, so insect development can proceed uninterrupted by low nighttime temperatures.

These masses of insects in turn benefit many birds that nest in northern Alaska, enabling parents to find food nearly 24 hours a day and providing juicy packages of protein to feed their hungry chicks. Insect-eating chicks grow faster and fledge sooner than similar-sized species nesting farther south, and females of some species such as hoary redpolls, snow buntings, and northern wheatears lay more eggs than their southern counterparts. Apparently long daylight enables the females to find food to provide the extra energy to lay more eggs, and allows both parents to gather enough food to feed larger families.

*Giant cabbages at the Alaska State Fair in Palmer,
Southcentral Alaska.*

Long summer daylight also benefits Alaska's fish. Studies of arctic grayling, which feed by sight, show that they feed 24 hours a day during June and July in Interior Alaska. They cease feeding later in the year only during darkness.

Arctic mammals may also benefit from increased daylight. Animals that feed by sight have more hours in which to feed. Highly nutritious, fast-growing vegetation benefits grazing animals such as caribou, which need to develop good body condition in summer to survive harsh northern winters and be fit enough to reproduce in the spring.

Benefits of the midnight sun and long hours of daylight are seldom lost on Alaska's human residents and visitors. There are few other places in the world where one can work all day and still have time after dinner to climb a mountain or catch a salmon—or

HOURS OF DAYLIGHT

MAXIMUM: SUMMER SOLSTICE (JUNE 20 OR 21)

	Sunrise	Sunset	Hours
Ketchikan	4:04 A.M.	9:33 P.M.	17:29
Fairbanks	1:59 A.M.	11:48 P.M.	21:49
Barrow	May 10	August 2	84 days

MINIMUM: WINTER SOLSTICE (DECEMBER 21 OR 22)

	Sunrise	Sunset	Hours
Ketchikan	9:12 A.M.	4:18 P.M.	7:06
Fairbanks	10:59 A.M.	2:41 P.M.	3:42
Barrow	—	—	0:00

(In Barrow, the sun does not rise above the horizon for 67 days.)

to raft a river, hike past a glacier, and picnic at sunset all within a single day. Those who appreciate solitude in nature can venture out after midnight or for a 3:30 A.M. sunrise and be rewarded with close looks at wildlife, which are more active during these early morning hours.

Where to See Alaska's Midnight Sun

Many tour companies operating out of Fairbanks offer bus, van, and airplane tours in summer to the Arctic Circle and beyond. On summer solstice, the longest day of the year, you can join local residents to watch the sun from traditional high-elevation viewpoints on Alaska highways. On the Steese Highway, viewpoints are at Cleary Summit, 20 miles northeast of Fairbanks; Murphy Dome, 25 miles northeast of Fairbanks; and Eagle Summit, 108 miles northeast of Fairbanks. On the Taylor Highway from Tetlin Junction, views are good from several high points on Mount Fairplay. Many communities hold late-night Midnight Sun celebrations—including a baseball game, fun run, and Midnight Sun golf scramble in Fairbanks. ■

© Jeff Schultz/AlaskaStock.com

A family enjoys Alaska's natural wonders on the Kenai Peninsula.

Suggested Reading

Alaska Geographic Society. *Alaska Geographic.* Quarterly publications offer a wealth of information on Alaska's natural wonders. Anchorage: Alaska Geographic Society.

Alaska Northwest Books. *The Alaska Almanac.* Portland, Oregon: Alaska Northwest Books, 1999.

Connor, Cathy, and Daniel O'Haire. *Roadside Geology of Alaska.* Missoula, Montana: Mountain Press Publishing Company, 1988.

Davis, Neil. *Alaska Science Nuggets.* Fairbanks: University of Alaska Press, 1992.

————. *Aurora Watcher's Handbook.* Fairbanks: University of Alaska Press, 1992.

Ewing, Susan. *The Great Alaska Nature Factbook.* Seattle: Alaska Northwest Books, 1996.

Graef, Kris Valencia, ed. *The MILEPOST:* 50th Edition, Spring '98-Spring '99. Anchorage: Morris Communications Corporation, 1998.

Lynch, Wayne. *A is for Arctic: Natural Wonders of a Polar World.* Buffalo, N.Y.: Firefly Books, 1996.

O'Clair, Rita M., Robert H. Armstrong, and Richard Carstensen. *The Nature of Southeast Alaska: A Guide to Plants, Animals, and Habitats.* Seattle: Alaska Northwest Books, 1992.

Pearson, Roger W., and Marjorie Hermans, eds. *Alaska in Maps: A Thematic Atlas.* Fairbanks: University of Alaska Fairbanks, Alaska Department of Education, and Alaska Geographic Alliance, 1998.

Pielou, E. C. *A Naturalist's Guide to the Arctic.* Chicago: University of Chicago Press, 1994.

————. *The World of Northern Evergreens.* Ithaca, New York: Comstock Publishing Associates, 1994.

Selkregg, Lidia, ed. *Alaska Regional Profiles.* Six volumes. Anchorage: University of Alaska Arctic Environmental Information and Data Center, 1975.

Sherwonit, Bill. *Alaska's Accessible Wilderness: A Traveler's Guide to Alaska's State Parks.* Seattle: Alaska Northwest Books, 1996.

Sierra Club. *Pacific Northwest and Alaska: Sierra Club Guides to the National Parks.* New York: Random House, 1985.

Simmerman, Nancy L. and Tricia Brown. *Wild Alaska: The Complete Guide to Parks, Preserves, Wildlife Refuges, and Other Public Lands.* Second edition. Seattle: The Mountaineers, 1999.

Steinhart, Peter. *Tracks in the Sky.* San Francisco: Chronicle Books, 1987.

Wayburn, Peggy. *Adventuring in Alaska.* San Francisco: Sierra Club Books, 1998.

INDEX

*Page numbers in **bold face** indicate photographs.*